Federal
Milk Marketing
Orders
and
Price Supports

Federal Milk Marketing Orders and Price Supports

Edited by Paul W. MacAvoy

Ford Administration Papers on
Regulatory Reform

American Enterprise Institute for Public Policy Research
Washington, D.C.

Paul W. MacAvoy is professor of economics at Yale University and an adjunct scholar at the American Enterprise Institute.

Library of Congress Cataloging in Publication Data

United States. Dept. of Justice.
  Federal milk marketing orders and price support.

  (Ford Administration papers on regulatory reform)
(AEI studies ; 176)
  A condensed and edited version of an earlier report
by the Dept. of Justice.
    1. Dairy laws—United States. I. MacAvoy, Paul W.
II. Title. III. Series. IV. American Enterprise
Institute for Public Policy Research. AEI studies ; 176.
KF1921.A843   1977   343'.73'076   77-15520
ISBN 0-8447-3276-1

AEI Studies 176

Printed in the United States of America

CONTENTS

FOREWORD

Early in 1975, I called for the initiation of a major effort aimed at regulatory reform. Members of my administration, and the Congress, were asked to formulate and accelerate programs to remove anti-competitive restrictions in price and entry regulation, to reduce the paper work and procedural burdens in the regulatory process and to revise procedures in health, safety and other social regulations to bring the costs of these controls in line with their social benefits.

My requests set in motion agency and department initiatives, and a number of studies, reorganization proposals, and legislative proposals were forthcoming last year. A number of these resulted in productive changes in transportation, retail trade, and safety regulations. Nevertheless, much remained to be done, in part because of the time required to complete the analysis and evaluation of ongoing regulations.

This volume provides one set of the analytical studies on regulatory reform that were still in process at the end of 1976. Necessarily, these studies would have undergone detailed evaluation in the agencies and the White House before becoming part of any final reform program. They do not necesarily represent my policy views at this time, but they do contribute to the analyses that must precede policy making. I look forward to the discussion that these papers will surely stimulate.

Gerald R. Ford

GERALD R. FORD

PREFACE

For more than forty years the dairy industry has been subject to three-tiered regulation by the federal government, involving price supports, surplus purchases, and quantity restrictions on the production of milk for home consumption. This regulation, designed to prevent collapse of the industry in the Great Depression, has been the subject of increased criticism as anticompetitive, wasteful, price-increasing, and even of questionable worth to producers. As part of a broad effort by the Ford administration to evaluate and reform regulation, the President's Antitrust Immunities Task Force was asked to study these regulations, since they were based on significant exceptions to the antitrust laws. In November 1975 the task force, which was at that time chaired by Thomas E. Kauper, assistant attorney general for antitrust, directed the Department of Justice staff to prepare a report on the effects of government regulation of the dairy industry. This volume contains a condensed and edited version of that report dealing with the impact on producers and consumers of the Department of Agriculture's regulatory practices in this area.

This is an important report for a number of reasons. Dairy products, and particularly fluid milk, are a significant ingredient in the American diet, particularly of young consumers and those in lower income groups. The market structure in this industry is not different from many agriculturally based retail industries, so that complicated and highly restrictive regulation applied here should provide an example of the effects that would occur in many other industries. The case for regulation here might apply to clothing, meat producing, and other "essential" industries in which the producers form a highly articulate and well-organized political group.

This study also has importance because of its comprehensive grasp of the intricacies of and results from a number of layers of regulation. Economic analysts in the universities and other organizations have done highly technical studies of specific aspects of behavior of the milk marketing order system and of milk cooperatives. A large number of studies have also been prepared by those within the industry, such as by those in trade associations, agriculture economic research bureaus, and the Department of Agriculture. The Justice Department's analysis, however, is the first comprehensive review of all aspects of regulation. The analysis is based upon an evaluation of the historical basis of the enabling legislation, the development of the dairy industry, and the mechanisms of "marketing orders" and price support programs. The study provides an evaluative process for determining the social costs and benefits of the entire system of controls, and it produces for the first time a rough estimate of the total costs and benefits of the system.

Finally, the study is important because the results contained in it move the debate on federal milk regulation forward one more step. The program is shown to be not only complicated but also extremely cumbersome, and it builds substantial inflexibility into the distribution of milk products in this country. The costs imposed on consumers and producers alike are substantial, and benefits are found to be insubstantial except for those who own the property on which the dairy farming takes place. Since consumers, farmers, and distributors do not benefit but landowners seem to be the ultimate recipients of the gains from a restrictive and complicated process, the case for continuing marketing orders and price supports cannot be made, and instead the compelling argument is that a gradual phased deregulation program should be undertaken.

PAUL W. MACAVOY
Yale University
November 1977

PROJECT STAFF

This report was prepared in the U.S. Department of Justice during the tenures of assistant attorneys general Thomas E. Kauper and Donald I. Baker by Antitrust Division staff Roger W. Fones, Esq., Janet C. Hall, Esq., and Robert T. Masson, Ph.D., subject to the immediate supervision of Donald L. Flexner, acting chief of the division's Regulated Industries Section and the overall guidance of Jonathan C. Rose, deputy assistant attorney general. Also contributing to the preparation and analysis of the report were A. Theodore Gardiner III and Vicki Golden, attorneys in the Antitrust Division.

1

PUBLIC POLICY TOWARDS THE DAIRY INDUSTRY

Two major pieces of federal legislation directly influence how milk is marketed in the United States today. These are the Capper-Volstead Act and the Agricultural Adjustment Act.[1] The former, along with section 6 of the Clayton Act, is the source of whatever antitrust exemptions exist for farmer cooperatives; the latter is the enabling legislation for the federal milk order system, the regulatory scheme under which most of the milk produced in the United States is marketed. It was concern over the competitive impact of these enactments, and over their effects which were not intended by Congress, that led to this study of milk marketing.

The existence of a degree of antitrust immunity for the cooperative form of business, coupled with the existence of regulation of milk prices and marketing by the federal government, has led to some restrictive behavior by industry participants as well as to noncompetitive markets for milk in many areas of the country. The discussion of many of the issues is applicable to other agricultural commodities, particularly with respect to the Capper-Volstead Act. Similarly, the Agricultural Adjustment Act authorizes marketing orders for other commodities in addition to milk. Milk orders, however, are the most comprehensive, and they are the only ones which set prices.

Overview of the Federal Milk Order System

The marketing of milk as it is known today is the result of the interaction between government regulation on the one hand and the activity of Capper-Volstead cooperatives within that regulated frame-

---

[1] When subsequently reenacted and amended, the Agricultural Adjustment Act was entitled the Agricultural Marketing Agreements Act.

work on the other. It is the federal milk order system, however, that particularly distinguishes dairying from other forms of agricultural endeavor and has contributed significantly to the local and regional concentration of control over the marketing of farm milk which is characteristic of the dairy industry today. For this reason, it is helpful initially to understand, in general, what the federal milk order system is, and how it works.

A federal milk order is a regulation issued by the secretary of agriculture. As such, it appears in the *Federal Register* and becomes codified in the *Code of Federal Regulations*. Current milk orders can be found in sections 1001–1159 of Title 7 of the code. Each milk order defines the geographic region to which it applies. Consequently, "order" is often used as a shorthand term for the "area to which an order applies."

Federal milk orders are administered by the Dairy Division of the Agricultural Marketing Service, which is within the U.S. Department of Agriculture (USDA). Each order has a local "market administrator," a government employee, generally located in the marketing area, who is responsible for operating the order, making audits, collecting and dispersing funds, making statistical reports of activity in the order, and similar activity.

The market order area is usually a region with similar production characteristics. It is common for an order to be centered around a population center and to extend outward to encompass what could be thought of as the "normal" supply area for the population center.

Once the geographic area is defined, the order regulates the milk dealers (called "handlers" by the orders) who sell their milk in the area. Federal orders only regulate the purchase of grade A milk by handlers in the market area. Grade A milk is simply that milk which meets local health and sanitation requirements for consumption in fluid form; ungraded milk (commonly referred to as grade B) may only be used for manufacturing purposes. Grade A may, of course, be used for any purpose.

The market orders regulate the minimum prices that may be paid by handlers for raw grade A milk and the prices received by the dairy farmers (called "producers" by the orders). These prices are *not* the same. Handlers pay *classified prices* for milk received. Classified prices are simply prices based on the class, or use, to which the handler puts the raw milk. Some orders have two classes of milk; most have three. Class I products generally include fresh whole milk, skim milk, milk drinks, buttermilk, and so forth. Class II products, often referred to as "soft" manufactured products, include sour cream, cottage cheese, and similar products. Class III products, called "hard" manufactured products, include such items as hard cheeses, butter, evaporated or condensed milk, and dry milk powder. Orders with only two classes of milk divide them simply into fluid and manufactured products. (For simplicity, this dichotomy will be used throughout this analysis, with the understanding that Class II can also mean Class II and Class III. The Class II price customarily exceeds the Class III price by 10 cents per hundredweight.) Regulated handlers (that is, handlers located in an order market area) must pay not less than a minimum fixed price for producer milk used for Class II purposes, and a higher, minimum fixed price for milk going into Class I uses. The Class II prices are fairly uniform in orders throughout the country; the Class I prices increase as the distance the order is from the Upper Midwest milkshed increases.[2]

Dairy farmers whose milk is sold to regulated handlers receive neither of these prices. Rather, they receive a uniform weighted-average, or "blend," price based upon how much milk goes into each class usage in the order. All of the proceeds for milk sales in the order are "pooled" and then divided so that each producer receives the same per unit price for his deliveries. This means that each producer receives a pro rata portion of the higher Class I proceeds. If 75 percent of the milk sold is sold for Class I use in the order, each producer receives total revenue that is equivalent to receiving the Class I price for 75 percent of his milk sales and the Class II price of 25 percent of his milk sales. Each producer receives this same blend price regardless of the actual use of his raw milk deliveries.

The above explanation of federal milk market order prices is highly simplified. Prices paid by handlers and received by producers are subject to numerous adjustments. These include location differentials, a butterfat differential, and seasonal adjustments. A location differential is an adjustment made depending upon the location of the buyer and the seller. The price received by a producer will be adjusted for the distance he must ship the milk to the handler, and the Class I price paid by a handler will be adjusted for the distance he is located from the market center, in order to compensate him for the cost of shipping his processed fluid products to market. The butterfat differential means merely that the price will vary according to the butterfat content of the milk delivered. Seasonal adjustments are of several types, but basically they are directed at paying the producer a higher price during the fall season when milk supply is short and a lesser price during the spring when cows normally give more milk.

The terms of each order specify exactly how much the minimum

---

[2] A milkshed is simply the "normal" supply area in a market.

price for Class I milk to be paid by handlers will exceed the minimum price for Class II. This difference is called the Class I (or fluid) differential. The differential is added to the manufacturing price for all milk used for fluid purposes.

How are the manufacturing (or Class II) price and the fluid (or Class I) differential for each order determined? The manufacturing-use price in each order is usually equivalent to the market price for grade B milk prevailing in the Minnesota-Wisconsin area. This price is computed monthly by the USDA. The manufacturing price is uniform throughout all order regions out of necessity: the market for manufactured products is national in scope. If the price for milk used in manufacturing was above the level prevailing in the highly productive areas of Minnesota and Wisconsin, cheese and other products would be shipped to higher priced areas, undercutting the competition.

The fluid milk market is in sharp contrast to this, with the contrast being reflected in Class I pricing policy. Unlike cheese, bottled fluid milk products are more expensive to transport than the raw milk from which they are made: raw milk has a much higher cost of transport-to-value ratio than manufactured products. In addition, manufactured products are not subject to as rapid spoilage as are bottled (fluid) and raw milk. For these reasons, the fluid milk market can be viewed as more localized than the manufactured milk product market. Although Class I pricing policy is a result of many factors, it can be said that one factor is that fluid milk markets are more local.

Before examining Class I pricing policy, it is important to note that, as a technological matter, fluid milk supply regions need no longer be local to the extent that they were during the 1930s when the Agricultural Adjustment Act was enacted. There are two geographic markets in which fluid bottlers compete: the market for their processed product and the market to which they turn for supplies of raw milk. Even today, the former is considerably smaller than the latter because bottled or packaged milk is more difficult to transport than bulk raw milk, which can be moved by tanker. Distribution of processed fluid products by handlers can cover a 250-mile radius, whereas raw bulk farm milk can be sold to handlers as far away as 2,000 miles.[3] However, both these markets are tremendously expanded from what they were in the 1920s and early 1930s. The technology of those years required prompt sale and consumption of milk products, limiting the supply and marketing areas to less than 50

---

[3] Alden C. Manchester, *Pricing Milk and Dairy Products: Principles, Practices, and Problems*, U.S. Department of Agriculture, Economic Research Service, Agricultural Economic Report No. 207 (June 1971), p. 3.

miles.[4] Although the technology has drastically improved the movability of milk, milk movements of the magnitude possible are uncommon. This is largely because the order system has operated to "freeze in" the local distribution system of the 1930s. In essence, the Agricultural Adjustment Act of 1933 took a snapshot of the milk markets of the Depression era and, against the pull of technological change, has maintained essentially local production and marketing of milk. The effect has been to prevent producers, handlers, and consumers from benefiting from a more modern and efficient marketing and distribution system.

This artificial localizing of markets is a direct result of Class I pricing policy. Each market order area is treated as largely autonomous, with the Class I price geared, purportedly, to local conditions: local costs, supply, and demand. According to the USDA: "In short, the Act requires the establishment of minimum prices which will equate the supply of milk with the demand *in each* regulated marketing area after making provisions for necessary reserve supplies."[5] Naturally, the Class I price must be higher in less productive regions if those markets are to be supplied by local producers. Because Class II prices are uniform throughout the country, raising the Class I price is the only means of raising the blend prices farmers receive in less productive markets. If prices in a less productive region rise above the cost of producing milk in an efficient area plus shipping costs to the less efficient area, then imports of raw milk will result. One solution to this problem is to raise Class I prices in the efficient areas as well in order to remove the incentive to ship milk out. This action has the direct side effect of encouraging excess production in the efficient production regions. Thus, to insure *local self-sufficiency* in all markets, prices in the least efficient market would first be set to insure adequate supply there, with Class I prices in markets decreasing to reflect the cost of transporting milk. According to the USDA: "Specified differentials to account for the additional cost of producing milk eligible for fluid use—and other special economic conditions, particularly transportation costs, which influence prices for milk in city markets—are added to the manufacturing milk prices."[6]

How does the scenario just described compare with what is observed in the market? In January 1976 the highest Class I differen-

---

[4] Ibid.
[5] U.S. Department of Agriculture, Agricultural Marketing Service, *Questions and Answers on Federal Milk Marketing Orders* (March 1975), p. 10 (emphasis added).
[6] Ibid.

tials were in Florida; the lowest were in Minnesota. Also, the Florida-Georgia region had the lowest surplus of grade A milk sold to handlers regulated by the orders involved. Generally, greater surpluses of grade A milk were found the closer the orders were to the Minnesota-Wisconsin milkshed.[7] This is exactly what would be expected. The extent of surpluses which exist in northern markets is a result of two factors: setting Class I prices in the southernmost market high enough to assure sufficient local production of grade A milk for local consumption, and then setting the Class I prices to the north no lower than necessary to reflect transportation costs of moving milk to the southern markets. The significant size of the surplus in northern markets reflects the magnitude of the cost involved in assuring *local* supply sufficiency, characteristic of the 1930s, in the least efficient production areas in the South.

An additional quirk of the federal order system with nationwide impact that bears noting is the classification of reconstituted milk as Class I.[8] The order system thus makes the cost to the handler the same for reconstituted milk as for fresh milk, thereby effectively keeping a product off the market. This classification removes any incentive for handlers to buy powdered milk from the Minnesota-Wisconsin area, ship it to less productive regions such as Florida at a fraction of the cost of shipping fluid milk, and then reconstitute it for sale. This is an example of how consumers have been denied the benefits of technological advances realized after the legislation was enacted. This problem is not dwelt upon at length in this report, not because it is unimportant or lacking impact, but simply because there is little more to add. It is simply another unfortunate result of attempting to legislate a marketing system.

The procedure for promulgating a federal milk order is fairly straightforward. The secretary of agriculture gives notice of a hearing when an order is being contemplated. Such a hearing, as a practical matter, results from a petition by producers through their cooperative. All interested parties may appear at such a hearing, and a recommended decision and proposed order result. A short period of time elapses so that comments and exceptions to the proposed order can be received, and a final order is issued.

In the case of a new order, a formal referendum, required by the statute,[9] is held. Approval by two-thirds of the producers selling

---

[7] U.S. Department of Agriculture, Agricultural Marketing Service, *Summary of Major Provisions in Federal Milk Marketing Orders, January 1, 1976* (February 1976), p. 55.
[8] Reconstituted milk is simply fluid milk re-created by adding water and fat to dried milk solids.
[9] 7 U.S.C., section 608c(19).

milk in the area covered (by either number or volume) who voted is required for passage.[10] Cooperatives are empowered to "bloc vote" for their members.[11] This means that a cooperative casts the votes of all its members regardless of a minority position within the cooperative.

If an existing order is to be amended, the required approval by two-thirds of the producers can be, and usually is, determined simply by contacting the management of the cooperatives involved. A milk order can be terminated by the secretary of agriculture if he finds either that the order no longer tends to effectuate the purposes of the act or that the termination is favored by a majority of the producers.[12] Currently, there are fifty-six orders, generally covering most of the population centers except for California.

As should be evident even from this cursory discussion, there is substantial intervention by the federal government in the marketing of milk through the operation of the federal order system. As mentioned at the outset, however, the marketing of milk is affected not merely by the order system but also by the operation of cooperatives within the order system. The cooperative form of farmer organization is an effective and reasonable means of creating some bargaining power in farmers when they enter the market to buy supplies or sell their raw milk. Historically and currently, farmer cooperatives provide valuable services to their members; they are and can continue to be effective and entirely appropriate bargaining forces. In addition, cooperatives have achieved some of the efficiencies that the Congress envisioned when it enacted the Capper-Volstead Act in 1922.

Within the last ten to fifteen years, however, problems have arisen out of the action of cooperatives within the order system. In some instances, there have been clear abuses by cooperatives acting well outside the scope of any reading of the antitrust immunity: in these situations, antitrust enforcement resulted. However, two other categories of cooperative conduct are more troublesome. First, the order system frequently provides an incentive for conduct which is either inefficient, economically irrational (but for the order system), or anticompetitive. This conduct is generally protected from the operation of antitrust laws by the order system. The second category of cooperative conduct, usually anticompetitive, is generally considered to be protected from operation of the antitrust laws, although

---

[10] Ibid., section 608c(9). In some cases, a three-fourths majority is required; ibid., section 608c(5)(B)i.

[11] Ibid., section 608c(12).

[12] Ibid., section 608c(16).

the extent of the immunity granted might be open to some question. Mergers of cooperatives provide a good example of this type of conduct, as do certain forms of joint action and anticompetitive agreements among cooperatives. In both categories, the impact of cooperative conduct upon and within the order system has been substantial, recurring, and in some cases harmful.

Legislative History of the Capper-Volstead Act

More than fifty years have passed since the passage of the Capper-Volstead Act.[13] There is little in the text of the Capper-Volstead Act to indicate precisely what sort of organization Congress intended to legitimize. In allowing farmers to cooperate and associate for the purpose of marketing their products, and in providing limited antitrust immunity for such activities, Congress seemed to leave unanswered many obvious questions concerning what powers these associations might exercise. What power, for example, did Congress intend to grant the cooperatives over the restriction and expansion of supply? And to what degree, if any, would the associations be free to merge with one another, creating larger cooperatives with correspondingly increased power over the market forces? An examination of the legislative history reveals less than definitive answers to these questions.

General Characteristics of an Agricultural Cooperative. The most consistent theme in the legislative history is Congress' intent to allow farmers to form some sort of association which would confer the advantages of corporate structure free from the threat of prosecution under the Sherman Antitrust Act. Congressmen debating the bill believed that the economic ills of the farmer could be cured, or at least alleviated, by allowing farmers to organize into cooperatives to equalize economic power vis-à-vis the corporations from which they had to purchase supplies and to which they sold their products.

> The farmer is a business man. It is most commendable and only natural that he would desire to use modern methods in the conduct of his enterprise. It is not fair that he should be denied the use of these methods. Cooperation is not "combination". . . . It is only through cooperation that the highest service to the public can be assured. This fact

---

[13] February 18, 1922, chapter 57, sections 1 and 2, 42 Stat. 388, codified at 7 U.S.C., sections 291–92 (1970).

is recognized by agriculture just as it is recognized by industry, finance, and commerce.[14]

Business men can combine by putting their money into corporations, but it is impractical for farmers to combine their farms into similar corporate form. The object of this bill is to modify the laws under which business organizations are now formed, so that farmers may take advantage of the form of organization that is used by business concerns.[15]

This legislation is primarily inspired by the desire to put the farmer in a condition, through cooperation and organization, where in some measure he may overcome the difficulties that inhere in his business . . . and *put him on an equal footing with all the other business men of America* and permit him in some measure to fix the price of the thing that he raises.[16]

Manufacturing industry can organize and form corporations without any thought upon the part of any human being that they are in violation of the Sherman antitrust law. They may control only the merest fraction of a percentage of a product; there may be no question of monopoly involved; but farmers can not organize and incorporate the business of farming as the business of manufacturing can be organized and incorporated. It is impossible to do so; and yet *today a group of farmers associating themselves together, and proposing to do the very thing that is perfectly legal for a corporation to do, stand in danger of being held to be in violation of the Sherman law.*[17]

In addition to giving the farmer some measure of economic power through joint action, it was felt that cooperation would benefit the ultimate consumer by giving the farmers countervailing power with respect to the "middleman." Organization was also seen as a means to allow farmers to integrate forward in the marketing process, displacing some middlemen. Further, it was felt that farm organiza-

[14] Remarks of Senator William M. Calder (Republican, New York), *Congressional Record*, vol. 62 (1922), p. 2217.

[15] Remarks of Congressman Andrew J. Volstead (Republican, Minnesota), ibid., vol. 61 (1921), p. 1033.

[16] Remarks of Congressman Charles F. Reavis (Republican, Nebraska), ibid., p. 1038 (emphasis added).

[17] Remarks of Senator Irving L. Lenroot (Republican, Wisconsin), ibid., vol. 62 (1922), p. 2224 (emphasis added).

tions would benefit the consumer by directing the farmer's energy toward research, increased production, and improved quality.[18]

Although the legislative history contains conflicting statements about whether there had ever been need for prosecution of farmer cooperatives,[19] the prevailing opinion in Congress was that farmers would organize into cooperative associations for the purpose of bettering their position *but for* the threat of prosecution under the Sherman Act.[20]

> But it is said that when advocates of the organization of these cooperative farm associations go about for the purpose of inducing farmers thus to cooperate and to associate themselves in cooperation for the purpose of marketing their products, interested parties, those who handled the business now, . . . and generally throughout the country the dealers in milk products, noise it about and circulate a rumor to the effect that organizations of that character are violative of

---

[18] Note the remarks of Congressman John M. Evans (Democrat, Montana): "Investigations of farm organizations are along the following lines: How can the yield be increased in quantity and value—how secure a better kernel, more kernels to the head or ear, more ears to the stalk, more stalks on the ground, better quality of flesh or meat, more of the better cuts to the single animal, more pounds produced from a given amount of feed and by using as little high-priced feed as is consonant with quality and economic production. His organization has directed its efforts towards increasing production and improving quality." Ibid., vol. 59 (1920), p. 7853.

[19] See, for example: Remarks of Senator Thomas J. Walsh (Democrat, Montana): "No prosecution, so far as the committee was able to ascertain, has ever been instituted under the Sherman Act against any organization of farmers except the proceedings brought against what is known as the California Raisin Growers Association." Ibid., vol. 62 (1922), p. 2122. Remarks of Senator William Henry King (Democrat, Utah): "I have made inquiry and am advised by the Department of Justice that only four prosecutions have been instituted under the Sherman antitrust law against what might be denominated agriculturists, and in each case there was a flagrant attempt to monopolize and to oppress the people." Ibid., p. 2276. Remarks of Senator William M. Calder (Republican, New York): "In some sections of the country, I am informed, officers and members of such organizations have been arrested, indicted, and even thrown into prison. United States attorneys and other officials have so construed the Sherman antitrust law as to make it cover the operations of nonstock, nonprofit farm associations." Ibid., p. 2217.

[20] Congress had placed itself in an awkward position in passing an appropriations bill under which $200,000 was appropriated for the enforcement of the antitrust laws with the proviso that "no part of this appropriation shall be expended for the prosecution of producers of farm products and associations of farmers who cooperate and organize in an effort to and for the purpose of maintaining a fair and reasonable price for their product." Thus, Congress appeared to be in the position of recognizing that farm organizations were in violation of the antitrust law but temporarily forbidding any prosecution of them. See remarks of Congressman Hugh S. Hersman (Democrat, California), ibid., vol. 59 (1920), p. 8025.

the Sherman Act and prosecutions are likely to be instituted if they are organized. Thus it is said . . . that farmers are deterred from associating themselves with these associations by reason of fear of prosecution under the Sherman Act.[21]

The Clayton Act,[22] passed in 1914 in part to make clear the legal status of labor and agricultural associations under the antitrust laws,[23] was thought inadequate to protect the farmers. The legislators debating Capper-Volstead perceived problems in the Clayton Act and confusion concerning what activities fell within the provisions of that act.

> The apparent intention of Congress, however, is not clearly expressed in section 6 of the Clayton Act, and it is rather uncertain what these farm organizations can lawfully do or what are "the legitimate objects thereof."[24]

In addition to problems created by ambiguities, the prohibition against capital stock limited the type of functions cooperative organizations could perform.

> The farmer of today finds that his associations must have capital stock in order to handle his business most effectively, and this bill is intended to legalize farmers' cooperative associations having capital stock. . . . The provision of the Clayton Act which permitted cooperative marketing among farmers can not under present business methods be fully taken advantage of, and this bill is framed in order to meet the situation that the farmers of this Nation are confronted with through the evolution of modern business methods.[25]

---

[21] Remarks of Senator Walsh, ibid., vol. 62 (1922), p. 2123.

[22] Act of October 15, 1914, chapter 323, 38 Stat. 730, codified at 15 U.S.C., sections 12–27 (1970). Section 6 of the Clayton Act stated: "That the labor of a human being is not a commodity or article of commerce. Nothing contained in the antitrust laws shall be construed to forbid the existence and operation of labor, agricultural, or horticultural organizations, instituted for the purpose of mutual help, and not having capital stock or conducted for profit, or to forbid or restrain individual members of such organizations from lawfully carrying out the legitimate objects thereof; nor shall such organizations, or the members thereof, be held or construed to be illegal combinations or conspiracies in the restraint of trade, under the antitrust laws."

[23] U.S. Congress, House, H. Rept. 627, 63rd Congress, 2d session, 1914, p. 14.

[24] Remarks of Congressman King Swope (Republican, Kentucky), *Congressional Record*, vol. 59 (1920), p. 8023.

[25] Remarks of Congressman Hersman, ibid., p. 8025. See also remarks of Congressman Swope, ibid., pp. 8022–23.

Thus, Congress intended that the Capper-Volstead Act authorize farmers to organize, so that farmers would enjoy the same benefits and powers that corporations they dealt with enjoyed.

Limited Powers of Agricultural Cooperatives. Although Congress intended that farmers be allowed to associate for the purpose of exercising countervailing power in their dealing with corporate entities, Congress did not contemplate that the organizations, in turn, would hold such a degree of market power that competition and the consumer would be adversely affected. When legislators and farmers in the 1920s spoke of cooperatives, they had in mind organizations largely local in nature, serving, as a large part of their function, the social needs of the community. These organizations were intended to possess and exercise only limited power to interfere with the competitive pricing of farm products.

It is clear that farm interests hoped to increase the percentage of the farm commodity dollar that went into the farmer's pocket, but neither the Congress nor the supporters of the Capper-Volstead Act contemplated that this would be accomplished either by raising prices to the consumer or by exploiting unreasonable market power. It was thought, rather, that the farmer's lot could be improved by forward vertical integration into marketing and distribution, the increased efficiency which such integration would entail, and improved access for the farmer to sources of market information. It was these functions which farmers' cooperatives were intended to fulfill.

Those supporting the cooperative concept hoped that, to the extent that the handling of commodities between producer and consumer could be taken over by organized producers, the total cost of distribution of agricultural commodities could be reduced, while returning a reasonable profit to the producer. The focus, then, was at least as much upon the efficiency gains of vertical integration as upon the gains in market power through horizontal combination.[26]

Finally, it was anticipated that farmers' cooperatives would serve as clearinghouses for information concerning the market for agricultural commodities. By the gathering of market information which could be accomplished only by a large organization such as a cooperative, it was felt that the farmer would be better able to protect himself against the superior knowledge of the marketplace of those with whom the producer had to deal: both suppliers and milk dealers.[27]

---

[26] See U.S. Congress, House, *Report of the National Agricultural Conference,* H. Doc. 115, 67th Congress, 2d session, 1922, pp. 24–25.
[27] Ibid., p. 10.

Congress, in allowing cooperatives to organize, was not seeking to foster monopolies. Some members of Congress were concerned about abuse by cooperatives, and other members were concerned about any language that would cut back on a cooperative's right to organize. To allay the concern of some about abuse, and to avoid potential interference with powers of organization, Congress struck on a compromise, which is the resulting Capper-Volstead Act. That compromise rests on an underlying sense that monopolies were undesirable and not to be countenanced, although there was disagreement about whether monopolization was likely to happen. If monopolization were to result, however, cooperatives would be subject to scrutiny by the secretary of agriculture who has the authority to determine if undue price enhancement has resulted.[28] It appears that in Congress' view, the cooperative, once organized, was intended to be largely subject to the same constraints as ordinary corporations.

There is some evidence, furthermore, that Congress was wary of any attempt to create and use market power beyond that *necessary* for the *limited purpose* of *offsetting corporate power*. Thus, Congress expressed concern about other potential abuses which it perceived. Its perceptions may be read as intending limitations on cooperatives.

Although the "persons" permitted to cooperate under the statute are not defined in the legislation, the legislative history indicates that Congress was legislating for the benefit of the small farmer who, by the sweat of his brow, produced the agricultural commodities necessary to feed the nation. Indeed, the report of the House Judiciary Committee stated that the "limitations [in section 1] are aimed to exclude from the benefits of this legislation all but actual farmers."[29] In the Senate the discussions centered around "men engaged in the collective sale and distribution of products which they themselves bring to maturity."[30]

Congress was concerned that persons other than the individual farmer, such as corporate interests, might increase profits at the expense of the consumer through the cooperative device. Thus, the Senate refused to amend the bill to include processors who by contract pay the producer of the agricultural product a price which depends upon the price which the manufacturer receives for the finished product.[31] This amendment was defeated because it was felt that it

---

[28] 7 U.S.C., section 292.

[29] U.S. Congress, House, H. Rept. 24, 67th Congress, 1st session, 1921, p. 1.

[30] Remarks of Senator Calder, *Congressional Record*, vol. 62 (1922), p. 2217.

[31] The amendment read: "And where any such agricultural product or products must be submitted to a manufacturing process, in order to convert it or them into a finished commodity, and the price paid by the manufacturer to the

would open the door to all manufacturers of agricultural products to elude the antitrust laws by paying farmers on a commission basis.

Conclusions. Although the legislative history of the Capper-Volstead Act is short on specifics, much of Congress' intent concerning the nature of agricultural cooperatives can be inferred from perceptions of the problems facing farmers, the way in which Congress saw the general nature of cooperatives, and the legislature's concern about areas of potential abuse. The cooperative which both Congress and Capper-Volstead backers foresaw was an entity possessing limited market power. Its activities were local in scope, as much social and educational as economic. This cooperative was concerned with increased efficiency achieved through forward vertical integration, as well as enhanced bargaining power vis-à-vis suppliers and milk dealers gained through horizontal cooperations. Moreover, repeated expressions of congressional concern indicate that the Capper-Volstead Act was not intended to foster monopolies, and that cooperatives were not granted the right to restrict supply. In short, Congress in 1922 intended to allow farmers to organize with limited powers for the purpose of counteracting a specific problem; it did not intend to create organizations to replace one system of adverse market conditions with another.

Congressional Response to the Depression: Agricultural Adjustment Act

By 1930, major fluid milk markets had health regulations which raised the cost of fluid milk over the cost of milk for manufacturing use (which had fewer or no health requirements). When the gap between the blend price of fluid and manufacturing milk prices surpassed the cost of upgrading milk to pass health requirements, there was a theoretical price advantage to convert production from manufacturing grade milk to fluid grade milk. The predominant dealer groups in most markets, however, had organized to fix the price paid to farmers for milk for fluid use long before farmer cooperatives had organized. The purpose of such action was to prevent any dealer from initiating price competition in the fluid milk market. It was the dealers who

---

producer thereof is controlled by or dependent upon the price received by the manufacturer for the finished commodity by contract entered into before the production of such agricultural product or products, then any such manufacturers may have the facilities and the opportunity of cooperating in the selling of their products as provided in this bill for the farmer himself." Remarks of Senator Lawrence Cowle Phipps (Republican, Colorado), ibid., p. 2227.

policed the cooperative classified pricing systems to prevent any dealer from obtaining milk cheaper than the other dealers. Thus, it was not possible for a noncooperative farmer to undercut the existing Class I price by offering his milk at a lower price to one of the dominant dealers. If there was evidence of significant quantities available at the lower price, the dealers might negotiate the price charged by the cooperative group downward. Group pressure prevented any dealer from making an agreement independent of other dealers. Thus, throughout the 1920s the price difference between fluid and manufacturing milk was maintained at a larger difference than the cost difference between producing fluid and manufacturing grade milk.[32] With the collapse of demand for ungraded milk and the introduction of equipment for small-scale pasteurization, this was no longer possible.

As early as 1928, farmer organizations began to develop means of controlling the total production of milk in their markets in an attempt to support the manufacturing price. The cooperative organizations found themselves unable to enforce such programs because of their inability to secure the support of all farmers in a given market. As long as some farmers remained outside an agreement to reduce or control production, the cooperatives would be thwarted because production by nonmembers would increase any time the cooperatives were able to raise the price of milk. In practice, the cooperatives recognized their weakness and attempted to get governmental assistance to bring supply and demand into equilibrium at a price level they thought equitable. Because of the interstate nature of milk movements in the major markets—both Chicago and New York City markets, for example, received milk from neighboring states—the cooperatives turned to the federal government.

Programs were introduced in Congress from 1929 to 1932 that were aimed at assisting the farm sector in general and dairy producers in particular through various schemes of export promotion, import restriction, and production allotments. By 1932 no action had been taken and the continuous decline in dairy and other farm prices forced a shift in the legislative goals of farm groups. The immediate need of farmers was for income support until programs could be developed to balance the supply and demand for farm products. The situation in the dairy industry became critical when farmers initiated a series of milk strikes to win higher prices for fluid-use milk. This approach only induced more dealers to lure milk away from cheese plants in

---

[32] Roland W. Bartlett, *Cooperation in Marketing Dairy Products* (Springfield, Illinois: Charles C. Thomas, 1931), pp. 17–30.

rural areas for shipment to urban areas to meet the demand for milk.[33] In Chicago unknown persons bombed country manufacturing plants which assembled milk for shipment into the Chicago market in defiance of the strike by the Pure Milk Association. Similar events occurred elsewhere.[34]

The dramatic deterioration in the market for dairy products is demonstrated by the rapid decline in price that occurred. As a percentage of parity[35] the prices for dairy products in 1929 were 103 percent of the parity price index for 1910–1914. By May 1933 dairy product prices had dropped to 61.7 percent of the 1910–1914 parity index. Moreover, the dairy farmer's problems were not limited to the marketplace. Farmers were faced with the effects of bank failures, and they experienced many mortgage foreclosures.[36] There was a startling increase in the number of farm exits, which only served to increase the already high rate of unemployment in the cities.[37] The failure of the agricultural sector was perceived as contributing to the failure of the industrial sector because the farmer, without money in his pocket, was unable to purchase farm equipment and farm consumer goods, thus leaving the city factories idle. Idle city workers in turn had no money with which to buy farm products. By 1933, with the drastic drop of dairy product prices, the situation had deteriorated to crisis proportions, and all sectors of the economy were looking to Washington for help.

By January of 1933 a heavily Democratic Congress and a Democratic President had been sworn in. The Democrats had run on a platform of getting the country out of the Depression. In debating the farm bill, the Democrats frequently criticized the former Republican President for doing nothing about the conditions that led to the Depression and making no effort to lift the country out of the Depression.[38] It is clear from the legislative history that many members

---

[33] See Hutzel Metzger, *Cooperative Marketing of Fluid Milk*, U.S. Department of Agriculture, Technical Bulletin No. 179 (May 1930), p. 11.

[34] George M. Beal and Henry H. Babken, *Fluid Milk Marketing* (Madison, Wisconsin: Mimer Publishers, 1956), p. 87.

[35] Parity price is defined: "One which would give a unit of a farm commodity (for example, milk) the same purchasing power, in terms of goods and services farmers buy, that it had at a specific prior period." Milk Pricing Advisory Committee, *The Milk Pricing Problem*, Report to the U.S. Department of Agriculture, Part I (March 1972), p. 6.

[36] Remarks of Congressman James Archibald Frear (Republican, Wisconsin), *Congressional Record*, vol. 77 (1933), pp. 688–91.

[37] Remarks of Congressman Ray P. Chase (Republican, Minnesota), ibid., p. 676.

[38] See, for example, remarks of Congressman Ralph Fulton Lozier (Democrat, Missouri), ibid., p. 691.

perceived the situation as one of crisis proportions requiring drastic measures to correct it.

The root of the problem was popularly perceived as one of a lack of purchasing power on the part of the farmer. "The present economic emergency is in large part the result of the impoverished condition of agriculture and the lack of the ability of farmers to purchase industries commodities."[39] With substantially depressed incomes, farmers could not buy equipment. Without farm purchases, city factories lay idle. Thus, consumers had no money to buy farm products. This led to the peculiar combinations of overproduction by the farmer, attempting to generate some income, and underconsumption, given the depressed prices, by the consumer. Thus, the Congress saw as their object to establish a balance between production and consumption of agricultural commodities.[40] Members of Congress expressed tremendous concern for the farmers' plight. It was uppermost in their mind that farmer income had dropped drastically from the 1920s level by the early 1930s. For example, one congressman noted that the farming income in 1929 was $11.9 billion, while in 1931 it was $5.2 billion.[41] Further, the middleman was perceived as the "bad guy," taking much of the price of farm products, and returning little to the farmer.[42]

In an atmosphere of crisis, President Franklin D. Roosevelt proposed a program of processing taxes, allotment plans, and licenses as a means of putting agriculture back on a sound basis. The processing-tax concept provided for the assessment of taxes upon the processor of agricultural products. This tax would be regulated by the secretary of agriculture in amounts necessary to pay for land leased from farmers, which lands would remain untilled for a season. This was an attempt to bring about a "proper reduction in production," which at the time was thought to require the removal of 50 million to 60 million acres of tillable land.[43]

The second major provision in the bill as proposed by President Roosevelt was an allotment plan. This plan also provided for a tax to be levied upon a processor, which would then be used to support the price of farm products at a 1909–1914 parity price level.

This tax levied and collected from the processor shall be added to the price that the farmer is now receiving for his

[39] U.S. Congress, House, H. Rept. 6, 73rd Congress, 1st session, 1933, p. 7.

[40] Ibid., p. 2.

[41] Remarks of Congressman John Andrew Martin (Democrat, Colorado), *Congressional Record*, vol. 77 (1933), p. 669.

[42] See ibid., vol. 77 (1933), p. 835, on limiting the profit of middlemen.

[43] U.S. Congress, Senate, S. Rept. 16, 73rd Congress, 1st session, 1933, p. 2.

products, thus giving him for that part of his products domestically consumed a price representing the parity that existed between what he sold and what he bought between 1909 and 1914.[44]

A minor provision of the 1933 act as proposed by the President provided for the issuance of licenses and marketing agreements by the secretary of agriculture. The Senate report deals with the marketing agreements and licensing provisions as a sort of supplemental approach to achieving the principles sought to be affected by the allotment plan.[45] The secretary was authorized at his discretion to issue licenses permitting processors to engage in the handling of a basic agricultural commodity. The licenses would be issued subject to certain terms and conditions, which terms and conditions were necessary to eliminate "unfair practices or charges" preventing or tending to prevent effectuation of the policy of the act.[46]

The marketing licenses and agreements provisions were "added somewhat hastily . . . in the latter days of the bills' evolution."[47] Dairy cooperatives were generally in favor of the marketing agreement and license provisions.[48] They felt the licenses "could be useful in remedying the two great weaknesses in prevailing cooperative efforts; namely, the failure of producers to give full support to their cooperative organization, and destructive price-cutting on the part of distributors."[49] The dairy interests accepted the final bill as a compromise: there were mixed feelings about the processing-tax provisions, but great interest in the agreement and license provisions.[50]

The bill was introduced by the President as an attempt to meet what was termed by him an "unprecedented condition" requiring emergency action.[51] The President characterized the bill as a temporary expedient, seeking to increase the purchasing power of farmers. Many members of Congress, expressing some reservation about the extreme powers delegated to the secretary, and whether the approach suggested by the President was the proper one, nonetheless agreed to go along with the bill because of their shared per-

---

[44] Ibid., p. 3.

[45] Ibid.

[46] Ibid.

[47] Edwin G. Nourse, *Marketing Agreements under AAA* (Washington, D.C.: The Brookings Institution, 1935), p. 1.

[48] Ibid., p. 197.

[49] Ibid.

[50] Ibid.

[51] U.S. Congress, Senate, S. Rept. 16, 73rd Congress, 1st session, 1933, p. 1.

ception that in fact the situation was an emergency one calling for a dramatic experiment in an attempt to achieve a satisfactory result.[52]

The Congress essentially accepted the President's bill. The purposes declared in section 2 of the act were threefold. The primary purpose of the bill was to improve the farmer's purchasing power. This was to be attained by achieving a price level for most agricultural commodities that was at parity with the base period, August 1909 to July 1914.[53] That period was chosen because it was perceived as a time when agricultural commodities were receiving a relatively high return. There was some discussion in the Congress that, at that time period, price levels for milk were depressed, and that a more appropriate time period for determining parity price levels for milk products would be the late 1920s.[54] However, an amendment to that effect was not accepted at the time the 1933 act was passed.[55]

There was critical discussion in Congress as well about using a parity concept as the mechanism for determining the price level to be achieved. Some congressmen felt that cost of production was the appropriate price level which the government should strive to maintain. However, this approach was eventually rejected.[56]

The second goal of the act was to achieve this appropriate price level gradually, in order to achieve the third purpose of the act, which was to "protect the consumers' interest." Congress wanted to raise the price of agricultural commodities through the various mechanisms outlined in the bill as quickly as possible, but without achieving a level which would exceed that which was considered appropriate, that is, parity prices.

The overall approach to achieve these goals was to bring production in line with demand. Since the marketplace during the Depression had been unable to stimulate an appropriate level of consumption in response to the greatly depressed prices, the Congress

---

[52] Remarks of Congressmen Frear and Lozier, *Congressional Record*, vol. 77 (1933), pp. 690–91. In fact, section 13 of the 1933 act as proposed by the President and as enacted, specifically provided that when the President determined that the emergency, as articulated in section 1 of the bill, ceased to exist, the President could declare the emergency ended, and essentially repeal the bill, retracting the powers granted to the secretary of agriculture. See Act of May 12, 1933, P.L. No. 10, chapter 25, title I, section 13, 48 Stat. 39, codified as amended at 7 U.S.C., section 613 (1970).

[53] Act of May 12, 1933, P.L. No. 10, chapter 25, title I, section 2, 48 Stat. 32.

[54] Remarks of Senator Royal Samuel Copeland (Democrat, New York), *Congressional Record*, vol. 77 (1933), p. 1426.

[55] U.S. Congress, House, H. Rept. 100, 73rd Congress, 1st session, 1933, p. 1 (Conference Report).

[56] *Congressional Record*, vol. 77 (1933), p. 3124 (vote by Senate to recede from Amendment No. 83, use of a cost-of-production standard: 48 to 33).

felt it necessary to manipulate production. The Congress chose a land-leasing program as the principal method. The secretary of agriculture was authorized to take farmland out of production by leasing it. The money necessary to implement the program was to be obtained by levying a processing tax upon the processors. This would in turn raise the selling price to the consumer: it was acknowledged that the tax would be passed on to the consumer.[57] Congress did not focus on the obvious decrease in consumption which would be brought about by higher consumer prices.

The second principal method used was an allotment plan. The government would pay a farmer a sum necessary to bring the price of his domestic "allotted" production up to the appropriate price level, that is, parity. Once again, the income necessary to support this program would be derived from a tax levied upon the processors. This was a very direct and quick method of assuring that the price received by farmers would be raised. The allotment plan and the land-leasing plan formed an integral program. The allotment payments, which were viewed as a necessary step to raising farmers' income, were likely to result in increased production, a result likely to aggravate the current conditions in agriculture. Thus, the removal of land from production through the leasing program was essential to controlling the probable production response to the allotment program.

The third method, marketing agreements and licenses, is not very clearly described in the legislative history, and it is dealt with very briefly in the act itself. The secretary was authorized to approve agreements and to issue licenses "to effectuate the purposes" of the allotment plan program.[58] There was some floor debate on the question of whether agreements and licenses should be entitled to antitrust exemption.[59] Many in the Senate thought that the antitrust immunity which would come with the secretary's approval ought not to be extended beyond those commodities designated as "basic." (Milk was designated a basic commodity.) However, the forces in favor of employing agreements and licenses for all commodities prevailed.[60]

The bill as enacted is extremely vague with respect to agreements and licenses. The 1933 act granted broad powers rather than any

---

[57] See U.S. Congress, Senate, S. Rept. 16, 73rd Congress, 1st session, 1933, p. 3.

[58] Ibid., p. 3.

[59] *Congressional Record*, vol. 77 (1933), pp. 3116–17.

[60] U.S. Congress, House, H. Rept. 100, 73rd Congress, 1st session, 1933, p. 2; remarks of Senator Ellison DuRand Smith (Democrat, South Carolina), *Congressional Record*, vol. 77 (1933), pp. 3116 and 3118.

specific mandate.[61] The act does not spell out the provisions to be included in the licenses or agreements. It was likely that Congress conceived that such agreements could include provisions on price.[62] The language of the bill did not, however, clearly articulate what provisions would be contained in agreements and licenses and how they might further the purpose of the act.

The powers proposed to be granted to the secretary were extremely broad and flexible.

> The act was so drawn as to allow the test of time to decide which type of approach should be used in a given situation or whether some combination of the two should be employed.[63]

In fact, licenses were never intended as "an end in themselves," but merely as a means to prevent unfair trade practices.[64] Because competitive price cutting was viewed in the early 1930s as unfair trade practice by organized handlers and cooperatives, the foundation was laid for the evolution of licenses into minimum price-fixing devices.

With the passage of a series of amendments in 1935, the order system, essentially as it is known today, was authorized. The key features of the order system today—voting by producers, fixing of minimum prices, bloc voting, payments to cooperatives, and the various provisions for differentials, both seasonal and locational— were all provided for in the 1935 act.[65]

Although the licenses authorized by the 1933 act could set prices and control milk marketing conditions, the 1935 act greatly refined the ideas of price setting and market controls as a means to raise producer income. In a book written about the time the 1935 act was passed, a noted agricultural expert made the following observation about the collective price making and controlled marketing of the order system:

> It has *many points of similarity with the cartel movement in industry.* Its general price theory is built upon the

---

61 Nourse, *Marketing Agreements under AAA*, p. 2.

62 See remarks of Senator Smith, *Congressional Record*, vol. 77 (1933), p. 3116.

63 Ibid., pp. 3116–17.

64 Statement of Secretary of Agriculture Henry A. Wallace, U.S. Congress, House, *Hearings on H.R. 3835*, 73rd Congress, 1st session, 1933, p. 130.

65 There is little revealed in the legislative record about why these specific approaches were taken. The only clue to the reason for them lies in the general statement of motivation: to avoid the problem of the *Schechter Poultry* case (which declared unconstitutional other New Deal legislation) and to avoid the misconstruction to which the 1933 act was subject. The overriding goal continued to be increased farmer income.

more aggressive elements of the cooperative marketing movement as that institution has developed over a considerable period of time prior to the passage of the [1933] AAA.

In the main, however, the practice which the cooperatives sought to perfect was not that of collective bargaining for a price but of collective control of the market movement of the commodity in order that certain price objectives might be reached or at least approached. Though the two procedures differ, the goal is the same.[66]

The order system of marketing control and price setting of which Edwin G. Nourse was speaking is startlingly close to the system still in use today.

Post-Depression Congressional Action

Since the late 1930s, there have been few changes in the legislative basis for marketing orders. However, some are worth noting. In 1965 steps were taken to alter the provisions of the milk marketing legislation with respect to differential payments, specifically to allow the implementation of Class I base plans. In the Food and Agricultural Act of 1965, Congress took steps that clearly recognized the ever-increasing dairy surplus and its constant downward pressure on prices.[67] The goal of the Class I base plan was to reduce surplus milk production and stabilize the income of dairy farmers in those areas governed by federal milk orders. It was clearly recognized that "excess production" was "uneconomic production."[68] Congress also felt that the plans might possibly decrease the costs to the Commodity Credit Corporation (CCC), a government agency which purchases surplus milk, in supporting a set price. The theory was that excess production would be curtailed, causing prices to remain above support levels, thus reducing the amount of expenditures required by the CCC to support the price of milk products.[69]

The theory of the Class I base plans is that they remove the necessity for dairymen to produce surplus milk in order to preserve their individual participation in fluid (high-price) milk markets.[70] A

---

[66] Nourse, *Marketing Agreements under AAA*, pp. 316–17 (emphasis added).
[67] The surplus problem is discussed in chapters 2, 3, and 6.
[68] U.S. Congress, House, H. Rept. 631, 89th Congress, 1st session, 1965, p. 7.
[69] See ibid.
[70] See U.S. Congress, House, H. Rept. 1123, 89th Congress, 1st session, 1965, pp. 1–2 (Conference Report).

1965 Senate report explains the effect Class I base plans might have:

> The dairy title would enable the producers in the Federal marketing order areas to tailor their production to the amount needed for fluid milk consumption. Milk for this year commands a higher price. At present this higher price and the lower price for milk used for other purposes such as butter, ice cream and non-fat dairy milk, are blended together and the producer gets a price reflecting both uses. Under the base plan he would be able to supply his share of the fluid market and get the higher price on what he produced. *This would enable him to discontinue producing for the lower price if he wished.* To the extent the producers in the higher cost fluid areas would utilize this provision, government surplus purchasing could be reduced.[71]

The concept of base surplus and base excess plans is relatively simple, once the federal market order system is understood. Each farmer is assigned, based upon some past representative production period, a "base," or volume, of production. In subsequent marketing years, the farmer is paid the Class I, or fluid-use, price for his base production. Production beyond his base volume would only yield to the farmer the Class II price, not the blend price. By limiting the base issued, the order can discourage excess, or surplus, Class II production.[72] There was opposition to the base surplus and base excess plans when they were introduced in Congress, principally because they were viewed as a means of erecting trade barriers between local markets.[73] That opposition does not, however, appear to have been substantial.

There are several other provisions of the Food and Agricultural Act of 1965 which should be noted. First, Congress enacted a provision specifically prohibiting bloc voting by cooperatives on the question of whether there ought to be a Class I base plan in an order. By a vote of fifteen to eight in the House Agriculture Committee, an attempt to delete the individual vote provision was defeated.[74] Fur-

---

[71] "Explanation of the Food and Agriculture Act of 1965," prepared by Senator Allen Joseph Ellender (Democrat, Louisiana), chairman, Committee on Agriculture and Forestry, U.S. Senate, 89th Congress, 1st session, October 12, 1965, p. 11 (emphasis added), contained in *Selected Legislative History Materials, Public Law 89–321, 89th Congress, H.R. 9811, November 3, 1965,* compiled by U.S. Department of Agriculture, Dairy Division, Program Analysis Branch.

[72] Remarks of Congressman Harlan Hagen (Democrat, California), *Congressional Record,* vol. 111 (1965), p. 20714.

[73] See, for example, remarks of Congressman Arnold Olsen (Democrat, Montana), ibid., p. 20922.

[74] Remarks of Congressman Paul B. Dague (Republican, Pennsylvania), ibid., p. 20710.

ther, to prevent producers in markets with Class I base plans from attempting to take advantage of the highest value of return for their base milk and then diverting their milk over the base volume to other markets, thus receiving a blend price on their surplus instead of the Class II price, the act provided for a reduction of payments to such producers to compensate for the diverted marketings and to assure equitable participation in the market.[75]

In 1970 Congress amended subsection 8(c) of the act so that it would be clear that seasonal adjustment plans and payments were a separate mechanism for production control from the Class I base plans.[76] In authorizing the Class I base plans in 1965, Congress had deleted the provisions specifically authorizing the seasonal adjustment plan payments.

Of the various pieces of farm legislation that have an impact upon the dairy industry, perhaps the most important in effect after the order legislation is the price support program. Price supports have been used as a means of providing a floor for the price of certain dairy products since the 1930s.[77] It became a full-fledged program during World War II because of the disruptive effect the wartime economy had upon the dairy industry. After World War II, the concern was that a long-range program be developed that would assure abundant production at fair prices. Congress perceived it to be in the nation's interest that production of sufficient supplies of food for this nation's needs be assured.[78]

After several temporary extensions of the price support programs implemented during the war, the Congress in 1949 authorized a permanent price support program.[79] The 1948 act, a temporary measure, had required the secretary of agriculture to support dairy prices at 90 percent of parity in 1949. The 1949 act, however, required that such prices be supported at a level between 75 percent and 90 percent of parity, as the secretary determined was necessary to assure an

---

[75] P.L. No. 89–321, section 101, in *1965 U.S. Code Congressional and Administration News*, pp. 1191–92; *Congressional Report* No. 1123, 89th Congress, 1st session, in *1965 U.S. Code Congressional and Administration News*, p. 4020.

[76] Act of November 30, 1970, P.L. No. 91–524, title II, section 201, 84 Stat. 1359, codified at 7 U.S.C., section 608c(5)(B)(Supp. V, 1975); U.S. Congress, House, H. Rept. 91–1329, 91st Congress, 2d session, 1970, pp. 18–19.

[77] See, for example, U.S. Congress, Senate, S. Rept. 16, 73rd Congress, 1st session, 1933, p. 4.

[78] H. Rept. 1927, 83rd Congress, 2d session, in *1954 U.S. Code Congressional and Administration News*, pp. 3399, 3402, and 3407 (Conference Report).

[79] S. Rept. 1130, 81st Congress, 1st session, in *1949 U.S. Code Congressional and Administration News*, pp. 2407–08.

adequate supply.[80] In April 1954, the secretary of agriculture dropped, rather abruptly, the milk price support level from 90 percent to 75 percent of parity. The secretary had been required to do so because the only factor to be considered in setting the price was what level would assure an adequate supply.[81] Responding to this action, Congress enacted the 1954 Agriculture Act which immediately raised the dairy price support level from 75 percent to 80 percent and added factors to be considered by the secretary in setting the price support level.[82]

The secretary is required to announce the support level for the next marketing year before the beginning of that year. The level may not be decreased during the year, but it may be increased (up to 90 percent of parity) if he determines the higher level is necessary. Such midyear increases have occurred. The CCC stands ready to purchase all qualified milk products (mainly butter, cheddar cheese, and nonfat dry milk) when offered at the support price. Such offers will be made when supplies exceed demand at prices above that level.[83]

Overview of Congressional Action

The authorization to organize granted to farmers by the Capper-Volstead Act and the substantial controls placed on the marketing of dairy products, together with the price support program, represent substantial government involvement in the dairy industry and deviation from the nation's economic norm of free enterprise. Review of the legislative history and of reports and analyses written at the time of the legislative enactments reveal substantial concern for the plight of the farmer, but little consideration of the long-run implications of the sum total of the different legislative actions. With the possible exception of the enactment of the permanent price support program in 1948, the other legislation was essentially enacted in a context of crisis and focused on short-run effects of the particular legislation under consideration. Congress' focus in the 1920s and 1930s was very much on the contemporary agricultural situation.

When Congress enacted the Capper-Volstead Act, it was re-

---

[80] U.S. Department of Agriculture, Agricultural Stabilization and Conservation Service, *Dairy Price Support and Related Programs: 1949–1968*, Agricultural Economic Report No. 165, p. 11.

[81] H. Rept. 1927, 83rd Congress, 2d session, in *1954 U.S. Code Congressional and Administration News*, p. 3421 (Conference Report).

[82] Ibid., pp. 3399 and 3421.

[83] U.S. Department of Agriculture, *Dairy Price Support and Related Programs: 1948–1968*, p. 11.

sponding to several conceptions about the agricultural marketplace. First, it saw a tremendous disequilibrium in power between the farmers and the corporations they had to deal with, both suppliers of farm goods and milk dealers. This disequilibrium was thought to place farmers at a substantial disadvantage in negotiating for the sale of their products, and thus to result in an inappropriate apportionment of milk sales revenues. Second, Congress was convinced by farmers and their representatives that authorizing cooperative associations was the answer to farmers' income and sales outlet problems. In the background all the while pressuring the Congress to act was the threat that cooperatives would be prosecuted.

Congress' response to this situation was to enact the Capper-Volstead Act which, simply stated, granted farmers the *right to organize* free from the threat of antitrust prosecution. Although the legislative history is vague about the precise functions and characteristics of these legalized cooperatives, Congress' intent in enacting the Capper-Volstead Act is clear. Congress allowed farmers to organize in order to equalize economic power vis-à-vis the corporations with which they dealt. Congress intended basically to grant to farmers the same advantage of collective action and the benefits of size enjoyed by investors in a corporation.[84]

When the Congress was confronted with the Depression, it expanded on the collective powers of cooperatives; it does not, however, seem to have considered the impact of cooperatives on the system of market controls which it eventually adopted. In 1933 the newly elected Democratic Congress and President were faced with a situation they described as an emergency of crisis proportions. Concerned about precipitous drops in farm prices, a sense of large numbers of farm exits adding to already high urban unemployment, and little demand for farm products, Congress felt that it was imperative to act. The sense of emergency suggests that the Congress' action in 1933 was one of desperation, and in a way it was. Congress was not unwilling to give to the secretary of agriculture extremely broad and vague powers.

The development of the order system illustrates the Congress' sense of desperation and its need to take some action. The original license provisions of the 1933 act were a minor element of the legislation, included by the President just prior to submission to Congress. Congress was concerned about several effects which it perceived to have resulted from the Depression. It was concerned about failures

---

[84] Some cases have interpreted "the marketing agencies in common" (MAC) language to grant farmer cooperatives a right not commonly enjoyed by corporations: to act in combination.

in farming and assumed they all resulted from depressed prices being insufficient to meet costs. Its analysis was not so refined as to focus on whether some or many of them were appropriate responses to changing characteristics of the industry, such as increasing efficiencies in size because of technological or marketing changes. In addition to the direct effect of low income on farmers, Congress was concerned about the indirect effect on the nation's milk supply: if income remained low, dairy farmers would continue to seek alternative sources of income, decreasing the nation's supply of milk.[85]

Thus, maintaining dairy farmers' incomes at a sufficient level was important to assure adequate supplies of an essential foodstuff. How the license provisions, or any part of the 1933 act, were to accomplish these general goals was not articulated, and was not likely understood. It was only after the cooperatives seized upon the license system as a solution to their view of dairy market problems, and after the threat of the Supreme Court declaring the 1933 act unconstitutional arose, that the outline of the order system as it exists today was developed. By 1935 the cooperatives had recognized the potential in the license/ order system, and some features of the 1935 amendments really represented a recognition by the Congress of the cooperative's role in the market order system. There is, however, no evidence in the legislative history of consideration or appreciation of how cooperatives could have an impact on the order system. Further, both the original Agricultural Adjustment Act and the amended version of 1935 were steps taken because of a crisis which gripped agriculture: something had to be done. In 1937 the Congress acknowledged a lessening of the crisis. Nonetheless, it continued the order system, with some amendments. There was little analysis of how a permanent order system, particularly with the impact of cooperatives, would affect the dairy industry in the long run. Nor was there any real appreciation, or even consideration, of how the order system and the cooperatives would interrelate.

---

[85] In the 1930s, supply continued to flow into a market from a relatively small geographic region.

2

THE DAIRY INDUSTRY TODAY

The characteristics of the dairy industry today offer a sharp contrast to the industry as it existed during the 1920s and 1930s. The marketing practices have become more integrated, the technology of the product has made significant advances, and the quantity of milk subject to various forms of economic regulation has increased.

Supply, Demand, Price, and Income Characteristics of the Dairy Industry

Two important aspects of raw milk have not changed over the years. The first aspect is that raw milk is still produced in two grades: grade A, that which is fit for human consumption in fluid form, and grade B, that which is only fit for manufacturing purposes. Grading standards are set by local health authorities. Grade B milk is slowly but surely disappearing. Under current regulations, farmers are encouraged to convert their farms to grade A farms in order to take advantage of the federally regulated prices applicable only to grade A milk. These prices currently return to the producer revenues in excess of the differences in costs between grade A and grade B production. In 1960, grade B accounted for 33 percent of all milk production; in 1965, 31 percent; in 1971, 24 percent;[1] and in 1974, 22 percent.[2]

---

[1] George C. Tucker, *Need for Restructuring Dairy Cooperatives*, U.S. Department of Agriculture, Farmer Cooperative Service, USDA Service Report 125 (July 1972), p. 18.

[2] U.S. Department of Agriculture, *Agricultural Statistics 1975* (1975), p. 371.

Most grade B milk is produced in the Upper Midwest, with 62.5 percent being produced in Wisconsin, Minnesota, and Iowa in 1971.[3]

The second aspect of raw milk that has not changed over the years has been its characteristic seasonal production cycle. Cows naturally produce more milk in the spring months than in fall, creating a relative shortage during the fall months. During 1974, production was up 12.7 percent for the year, while in November it was 9.9 percent below the average.[4] Although this is a considerable variation, technological advancements have made the variability much less than it used to be. Data for the years 1933 through 1944 for Wisconsin revealed an average intrayear variability of 74.6 percent in milk production,[5] as compared to 49.7 percent in 1973.[6]

Demand. The demand for grade A milk fluctuates greatly within a week. Demand by processors usually peaks on Thursday, with the lows occurring on Saturday and Sunday. Milk processed on Thursday and Friday can be on store shelves for weekend shoppers.[7] The decline in home delivered milk has contributed to the variability of the intraweek demand for grade A milk. Intraweek demand has now conformed to consumers' shopping patterns, which is concentrated on weekends. This is largely because the price of milk to handlers is the same regardless of the day purchased. Federal regulation offers no off-peak price incentives, so naturally handlers operate solely in anticipation of consumer shopping patterns.

Consumer purchases of fluid milk items in federal milk order regions also vary considerably from month to month. During 1974, peak consumption occurred in October, after school resumed. The low demand occurred in June. June sales were 10.3 percent below the year's monthly average, while the October sales were 5.5 percent

---

[3] Truman F. Graf and Robert E. Jacobson, *Resolving Grade B Conversion and Low Class I Utilization Pricing and Pooling Problems*, University of Wisconsin-Madison, College of Agricultural and Life Sciences, Research Division, R2503 (June 1973), p. 71.

[4] U.S. Department of Agriculture, Economic Research Service, *Dairy Situation*, DS-358 (December 1975), p. 5.

[5] Noel G. Stocker and Irwin R. Hedges, *Base-Surplus Plan in the Madison, Wisconsin Milk Market*, U.S. Department of Agriculture, Farm Credit Administration, Miscellaneous Report 136 (December 1949), p. 16.

[6] U.S. Department of Agriculture, Statistical Reporting Service, *Prices Received by Farmers: Manufacturing Grade Milk in Minnesota and Wisconsin, 1972–74* (July 1975), p. 6.

[7] National Commission on Food Marketing, *Organization and Competition in the Dairy Industry*, Technical Study No. 3 (June 1966), p. 165.

above the average.[8] In 1970, sales hit bottom in July and again peaked in October. The July sales were down 8.5 percent, while the October sales were up 6.9 percent.[9] Purchases were more stable in the peak months in 1966. Sales were lowest again in July, 9.1 percent below average, while March was the peak month, only 4.1 percent above average. Demand was fairly stable September through April of 1967, dropping off heavily during the summer months.[10]

Additional factors to be considered in understanding the demand patterns of the dairy industry today are the changes that have taken place in the marketing of dairy products. Door-to-door sales have decreased significantly. In 1954, more than half of all retail sales of fluid milk products were home-delivered. By 1971, less than 20 percent was purchased this way;[11] the figure is estimated at 7 percent for 1975.[12] Convenience stores have taken up some of the slack. This trend has been accompanied by a reduced brand consciousness on the part of consumers. Fluid milk is now seen as a highly fungible product. Supermarket and convenience store chains are increasingly integrating backward into dairy product processing, taking advantage of this consumer attitude.[13]

Consumer tastes are also changing, as reflected in consumption patterns over the years. In the years 1954 through 1972, consumption of plain whole milk stayed fairly constant, but low-fat and skim milk both increased dramatically. Filled and imitation milk have also found a market since 1965. Flavored milk and milk drinks have shown an increased consumption level; buttermilk consumption remained stable.[14] Other distinct trends include a drop in the consump-

---

[8] U.S. Department of Agriculture, Agricultural Marketing Service, *Federal Milk Order Market Statistics, Annual Summary for 1974* (June 1975), p. 82. (Hereinafter cited as *FMOMS*. These statistical compilations are published monthly and annually.)

[9] U.S. Department of Agriculture, *FMOMS, Annual Summary for 1971* (June 1972), p. 88.

[10] U.S. Department of Agriculture, *FMOMS, Annual Summary for 1967* (May 1968), p. 90.

[11] Alden C. Manchester, *Sales of Fluid Milk Products, 1954–72*, U.S. Department of Agriculture, Economic Research Service, Marketing Research Report No. 997 (June 1973), p. 6.

[12] Letter from Robert March, Dairy Division, Agricultural Marketing Service, U.S. Department of Agriculture, to Janet Hall, Antitrust Division, U.S. Department of Justice, June 2, 1976.

[13] Russell C. Parker, *Staff Report to the Federal Trade Commission, Economic Report on the Dairy Industry* (March 19, 1973), chapter 6.

[14] Manchester, *Sales of Fluid Milk Products, 1954–72*, p. 3.

tion of cream, and substantial increases in the consumption of sour cream and dips, yogurt, and eggnog.[15]

Supply. Like monthly consumption, monthly production of milk as measured by producer deliveries to federally regulated handlers varies considerably from month to month. Unfortunately, the variation pattern of supply does not match the variation of demand. Production generally peaks in the spring, usually May, and is at a low in the fall or winter. Table 2-1 summarizes this pattern since 1965. In 1975, the peak production was in May, 12.7 percent above the monthly average. In February of that year, it was 8.2 percent below the average. In 1970, the February production was down 8.8 percent, the May production was up 11.6 percent. In 1965, the peak was again in May, 13.8 percent above the average, while the low point occurred in September that year, 8.3 percent below the average. Since 1965, milk production has, if anything, become slightly more variable in federally regulated markets.

Supply, utilization, and price relationships in federal milk order markets have been the subject of some interesting trends over recent years. The trend in the increased supply of grade A milk has been pointed out above. At the same time, the utilization rate, that is, the percentage of grade A milk used in Class I (fluid) products has been dropping. Utilization rates have always been much lower in areas like Chicago, which is in the heart of the nation's milkshed, while less productive areas farther from Wisconsin and Minnesota have always had higher utilization rates, reflecting the fact that most production either goes into the primary milk products, or in some cases (for example, Appalachia) is exported further south to the less efficient regions. Even so, the trend in the national utilization rate has been downward, as can be seen from Table 2-2 and Figure 2-1. In 1965, the all-market utilization rate was 63 percent.

In 1975, the all-market utilization rate was 58 percent, while the Chicago area dropped to 36 percent and the Southeastern Florida area was 91 percent. A national utilization rate of 58 percent means that less than three-fifths of grade A production is needed for fluid uses. Stated simply, there is 72 percent more grade A milk being produced than was necessary to meet the demand for fluid products for which only grade A milk can be used. This surplus has become one of the serious problems milk regulators must deal with.

As the sanitation requirements for grade A milk become more strict, the additional costs of producing grade A milk become less. This also has a tendency to encourage more grade A milk production.

---

[15] Ibid., p. 5.

Table 2-1

VARIABILITY OF THE VOLUME OF PRODUCER MILK MARKETED UNDER FEDERAL ORDERS, 1965–1975

(volume in millions of pounds)

Year	High		Low		Monthly Average	Percentage Variation from Average
	Month	Volume	Month	Volume		
1975	May	6,502	February	5,298	5,771	20.9
1974	May	6,333	February	5,082	5,648	22.1
1973	May	6,270	November	4,983	5,518	23.3
1972	May	6,415	November	5,163	5,727	21.9
1971	May	6,274	February	5,143	5,642	20.0
1970	May	6,042	February	4,939	5,413	20.4
1969	May	5,737	November	4,759	5,086	19.2
1968	May	5,190	February	4,492	4,704	10.3
1967	May	5,010	September	4,165	4,476	18.9
1966	May	4,926	November	4,031	4,418	20.3
1965	May	5,162	September	4,160	4,537	22.1

Source: U.S. Department of Agriculture, Agricultural Marketing Service, *Federal Milk Order Market Statistics*, annual summaries, 1965–1975.

Table 2-2

UTILIZATION RATES IN FEDERAL ORDER
MILK MARKETS, 1965–1975

Year	All Markets	Chicago	Southeastern Florida
1965	63	44	87
1970	62	45	92
1974	58	39	93
1975	58	36	91

Source: U.S. Department of Agriculture, *Federal Milk Order Market Statistics,* annual summaries, 1965–1975.

To the extent that average blend prices exceed grade B prices plus the cost of converting from grade B production to grade A production, more grade A production is encouraged. According to Truman F. Graf and Robert E. Jacobson, the cost of converting a grade B operation to a grade A operation in 1971 was thought to be 15 cents per hundredweight.[16] The average M-W price for 1971 was $4.81 per hundredweight.[17] This reflects the market price of grade B milk in the Minnesota-Wisconsin area. The "blend" price for the same year for federal order (grade A) milk in Minneapolis-St. Paul was $5.33 per hundredweight, a difference of 52 cents per hundredweight.[18] In 1975, the difference between the M-W price and the fluid-use price bottlers must pay (known as the "fluid differential") was $1.06 for the Minneapolis-St. Paul order.[19] If the Graf and Jacobson estimate is accurate, the difference between the price of grade B and grade A milk in the Minnesota-Wisconsin area was well above that necessary to encourage a producer to convert from grade B to grade A production, and it is not surprising that utilization rates would be dropping.

Milk production traditionally has been, and still is, widely dispersed geographically. The 1969 Census of Agriculture reveals that

[16] Graf and Jacobson, *Resolving Grade B Conversion and Low Class 1 Utilization Pricing and Pooling Problems,* p. 60.

[17] U.S. Department of Agriculture, *FMOMS, Annual Summary for 1972* (June 1973), p. 75. The M-W price (Minnesota-Wisconsin manufacturing grade price series) is computed monthly by the Department of Agriculture and is the average price paid by buyers for grade B milk in the Minnesota-Wisconsin area for the previous month. This price is the base price upon which the price structure of the federal milk order system is based.

[18] Ibid., p. 44. The blend price is the price received by the farmer.

[19] U.S. Department of Agriculture, Agricultural Marketing Service, *Summary of Major Provisions in Federal Milk Marketing Orders, January 1, 1976* (February 1976), p. 55.

Figure 2-1

CLASS I UTILIZATION IN FEDERAL MILK ORDER MARKETS
1965–1975

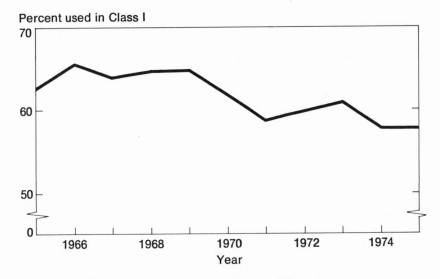

Percent used in Class I

Year

Source: U.S. Department of Agriculture, Agricultural Marketing Service, *Federal Milk Order Market Statistics*, annual summaries, 1965–1975.

the North Central area of the country produced 43 percent of the total dollar volume of dairy products, followed by the Northeast which produced 22 percent, the South with 21 percent, and the West with 14 percent. After the 1964 census, only the South increased its percentage of dollar value of total dairy products sold. Although production of milk suitable for fluid use is widely dispersed, the total production of manufacturing grade milk is highly concentrated in the Upper Midwest. Three states—Wisconsin, Minnesota, and Iowa— accounted for 62.5 percent of total manufacturing grade milk sold in the United States in 1971. Those same three states accounted for only 17.5 percent of total fluid grade milk sold in the United States during that year. No other state accounted for as much as 5 percent of the total manufacturing grade milk sold.[20]

The size of the local geographic market has been increasing, at both the wholesale and the retail levels. The area over which han-

---

[20] Graf and Jacobson, *Resolving Grade B Conversion and Low Class I Utilization Pricing and Pooling Problems*, p. 71.

35

dlers solicit raw milk supplies has increased. According to Alden C. Manchester, bulk milk now moves as far as 2,000 miles, packaged fluid milk moves 200–250 miles.[21] The increased transportability of fluid milk (raw or processed) is reflected in the trend toward fewer and larger market orders, and toward mergers of orders such as recently occurred in Texas. Ultimately, the geographic perimeter of supply areas is determined by price relationships between them. Because prices are delicately aligned, market regions can fluctuate. For this reason, discussions of "local markets" is an imprecise exercise.

A development that has impeded the transportability of raw milk has been the skyrocketing cost of fuel in recent years. The estimated cost per hundredweight per load-mile for transporting raw bulk milk in an over-the-road bulk transport trailer with one driver operating seven days a week during 1969 was 29.4 cents for a trip of 25 miles. This figure dropped to 15.2 cents per load-mile for trips of 125 miles and gradually leveled off as the distance increased to 13 cents per mile.[22] Of course, higher fuel costs now have driven costs of transporting anything much higher. The cost of transporting bulk milk is now probably in the neighborhood of 22 cents per load-mile for the longer distances. Transportation costs become very important in determining what prices should be charged in different milk markets under federal regulation, as Class I prices are now aligned to reflect transport costs of the late 1960s.

Prices. The prices of milk products have also been subject to trends in recent years. As might be expected, the general trend has been upwards. The M-W price for manufacturing grade milk has gone from $3.27 in 1965 to $4.66 in 1970 and $7.62 in 1975.[23] Although some of this increase may be associated with increasing the support levels for dairy products, the overall trend is significant and clear. Since the M-W price is the base price upon which federal order classified prices ultimately depend, Class I and II prices in federal order markets would follow similar trends to the M-W price. In 1975, the marketwide Class I price was $9.36, the high being $10.41 in the Southeastern Florida market order, and the low being $8.33 in Min-

[21] Alden C. Manchester, *Pricing Milk and Dairy Products: Principles, Practices, and Problems*, U.S. Department of Agriculture, Economic Research Service, Agricultural Economic Report No. 207 (June 1971), p. 3.
[22] Herbert H. Moede, *Over-the-Road Costs of Hauling Bulk Milk*, U.S. Department of Agriculture, Economic Research Service, Marketing Research Report No. 919 (January 1971), p. 8.
[23] U.S. Department of Agriculture, *FMOMS*, annual summaries for 1966, 1970, and 1975, pp. 87, 75, and 75, respectively.

neapolis-St. Paul.[24] In addition to the upward price trends in federal order markets flowing directly from the increase in the M-W price, there have also been increases in the Class I differential in federal order markets. In 1967, the Class I differential in the Minneapolis-St. Paul market order was 76 cents per hundredweight.[25] The following year it was 86 cents,[26] and in 1969 it was $1.06,[27] the level at which it has remained to the present.[28] The current fluid differential for Southeastern Florida is $3.15, the national high.[29]

In addition to the federal market order minimum Class I prices, handlers frequently pay prices in excess of the Class I price to dairy cooperatives. These payments may be monopolistic charges based upon the market power of the cooperative, a charge for services offered by the cooperative, or charges reflective of a local market shortage. According to USDA statistics which compare federal order Class I prices with announced cooperative Class I prices in thirty-one selected cities on a month-by-month basis between October 1973 and February 1976, the simple average over-order payment has ranged between 9 cents in February 1976 and $1.10 in September 1974.[30] Since October 1973, the difference between the federal order Class I price and the cooperative Class I price in those thirty-one cities has varied considerably between those two extremes. Data between 1966 and 1974 on the difference between the federal order Class I price and the dealer's average buying price for milk used in Class I products—that is, the average for all dealers in all markets whether buying from a cooperative or not—fluctuated between 16 cents and 33 cents between 1966 and 1973, going up to 45 cents in 1974.[31] A statistical

---

[24] U.S. Department of Agriculture, FMOMS, December 1975 Summary (February 1976), p. S2-3.

[25] U.S. Department of Agriculture, Consumer and Marketing Service, Summary of Major Provisions in Federal Milk Marketing Orders, January 1, 1967 (February 1967), p. 52.

[26] U.S. Department of Agriculture, Consumer and Marketing Service, Summary of Major Provisions in Federal Milk Marketing Orders, January 1, 1968 (February 1968), p. 53.

[27] U.S. Department of Agriculture, FMOMS, Annual Summary for 1969 (June 1970), p. 56.

[28] U.S. Department of Agriculture, Agricultural Marketing Service, Summary of Major Provisions in Federal Milk Marketing Orders, January 1, 1976, p. 55.

[29] Ibid., p. 56.

[30] U.S. Department of Agriculture, Agricultural Marketing Service, Federal Order Class I Prices and Announced Cooperative Class I Prices in 31 Selected Cities, October 1973–June 1976 (1976).

[31] Report of the Interagency Task Force, Price Impacts of Federal Market Order Programs, U.S. Department of Agriculture, Farmer Cooperative Service, Special Report No. 12 (January 1975).

analysis of USDA data[32] was done by the Department of Justice to determine if there was a correlation between the market share of the dominant cooperative and the amount of over-order charges in federal order markets. The results showed that for 1973 through 1975 there was less than a one-in-ten-thousand chance of an underlying causal connection not existing between the two. The higher the cooperative's share of the market, the higher and greater the incidence of over-order payments.

Retail prices of whole fluid milk have also shown a steady trend upward, especially in the past couple of years. For the most part, milk prices have moved with the price level of food in general, which since 1967 has moved up higher than consumer prices in general.[33] In 1965, a half-gallon of whole fluid milk cost the consumer just over 46 cents. In 1972, the price was still under 60 cents.[34] A big jump came in 1973 and 1974. In October of 1974, the average price of a half gallon of fluid whole milk was 77.5 cents.[35] The price level has been fairly stable since that time.

Income. Data on the income of milk producers are difficult to obtain and equally difficult to interpret. Data from Wisconsin suggest that operators of larger dairy farms earned upwards of $15,000 per year in 1974, not including return on investment or capital appreciation. Return on dairy farm investment was in the modest range of 5 percent to 8 percent between 1972 and 1974. This was below the all-farm average in 1972, above it in 1974.

These figures probably understate the dairy farmer's true income situation, since labor income and return on investment together represent total income. A permissible conclusion based upon what little data are available seems to be that over the long run dairymen earn about a competitive return on their labor and investment, although returns reflect a long-term trend to fewer farm units as technological change raises productivity. It is unlikely, however, that milk production provides many opportunities for making more than a competitive wage because of the fairly low entry barriers. Still, the larger farms, 50–100 cows, seem to be somewhat more profitable, which indicates some scale economies and reveals where the higher incomes are to be

---

[32] U.S. Department of Agriculture, Agricultural Marketing Service, Dairy Division, "Percentage of Producers Belonging to Cooperative Associations, Percentage of Producers Belonging to Dominant Cooperative and Weighted Over-Order Payments on Class I Milk, by Federal Order Markets," for 1973–1975.

[33] U.S. Department of Agriculture, *Agricultural Statistics 1973* (1973), p. 570.

[34] Ibid., p. 380.

[35] U.S. Department of Agriculture, *Dairy Situation*, DS-358 (December 1975), pp. 13–14.

made. Data on the trend in dairy farm size characteristics reveal that dairy farms are getting larger,[36] a fact that buttresses the notion that the larger farms are more profitable.

Fluid milk processing, like dairy farming, appears to be a business of marginal profitability, according to a recent report of the Federal Trade Commission. Between the third quarter of 1972 and the first quarter of 1975, after-tax profit as a percentage of stockholder equity averaged 7.7 percent for firms with less than $10 million in assets, 5.1 percent for larger farms.[37] A caveat must be added that the largest fluid milk processing firms do not specialize in fluid milk processing and hence were not included in the sample.[38]

Economic Regulation of Milk Marketing

As both the production and the processing of dairy products have continued to become more concentrated, the amount of milk subject to economic regulation has been increasing. In addition to federal market order regulation, milk marketing is also affected by the price support system, import quotas, and regulation of milk marketing by state agencies. Currently, all states have some form of regulation of milk marketing, at either the federal or the state level.

Federal Order Regulation of Milk Marketing. At the end of 1975 there were fifty-six federal milk marketing orders under which were marketed more than 69 billion pounds of producer milk, representing about 80 percent of all fluid grade milk produced. The number of separate federal milk order markets peaked in 1962 at eighty-three. Since that time the number of markets has been steadily declining, while the volume of milk regulated has been steadily increasing (see Table 2-3).[39]

The recent trend has clearly been toward fewer, larger milk market order regions. This reflects the fact that the technology of milk has advanced to the point where raw milk markets need not necessarily be local, as milk can be shipped great distances without spoil-

---

[36] U.S. Department of Agriculture, Economic Research Service, *The Impact of Dairy Imports on the U.S. Dairy Industry*, A Report for the U.S. Congress, Senate, Committee on Agriculture and Forestry, 93rd Congress, 2d session, January 2, 1975, p. 8.

[37] Alison Masson and Russell C. Parker, *Price and Profit Trends in Four Food Manufacturing Industries*, Federal Trade Commission, FTC Report No. R-6-15-25 (July 1975), p. 54. This report was not adopted by the commission.

[38] Ibid., p. 26.

[39] U.S. Department of Agriculture, *FMOMS, December 1975 Summary*, p. 9.

Table 2-3

MILK REGULATED BY FEDERAL MARKET ORDERS, 1950–1975

	1975	1970	1965	1960	1950
Number of orders	56	62	73	80	39
Volume (billion pounds)	69.1	65.1	54.4	44.8	18.6

Sources: U.S. Department of Agriculture, *Federal Milk Order Market Statistics, Annual Summary for 1974* (June 1975), and *December 1975 Summary* (February 1976).

ing. Despite technological advances, most milk markets are still *in fact* fairly local, largely because federal regulations have operated to "freeze in" the local character of the market system of the 1930s. (The local area has expanded, but it has been based on shipments of fluid product, not on availability of adequate potential supplies of raw milk.) In 1974, forty-three federal orders received more than 95 percent of their milk from either the state in which the order existed or an adjacent state.[40] This represented 73 percent of the producers' milk delivered to regulated handlers in federal order markets. Only seven orders received more than 10 percent of their milk from farther away than an adjacent state; in three of these orders, the supplying state was Minnesota.[41] A study of milk marketing done in 1967 revealed that between 85 percent and 90 percent of intermarket bulk milk shipments originated in cooperative supply plants and 90 percent of intermarket shipments originated in only twelve market areas.[42]

In 1974, of all fluid grade milk marketed, 78 percent was sold in federal orders. In 1965, this figure was 70 percent; in 1957, it was 53 percent. As a percentage of all milk sold (grade B milk included) these figures were 63 percent, 48 percent, and 34 percent, respectively.[43] No grade B milk is sold under federal market orders.

[40] Compiled from data appearing in U.S. Department of Agriculture, *FMOMS, July 1975 Summary* (September 1975), pp. 38–40.

[41] Ibid. Additional shipments that come from more distant sources as interorder *handler* shipments carry a consequent price disadvantage.

[42] W.D. Dobson and E.M. Babb, *An Analysis of Alternative Price Structures and Intermarket Competition in Federal Order Milk Markets*, Purdue University Agricultural Experiment Station, Research Bulletin No. 870 (December 1970), p. 5.

[43] U.S. Department of Agriculture, *FMOMS, Annual Summary for 1975* (June 1976), p. 9.

The Price Support Program. The price support program is separate from, but related to, the federal market order program. The Commodity Credit Corporation (CCC) is authorized to purchase manufactured dairy products in order to keep the M-W price at a predetermined support level. The support level is announced as a certain percentage of the parity price, which is defined by statute.[44] This support price has risen from $3.15 per hundredweight in 1964 to $4.93 in 1973 and finally to $7.24 in 1975.[45] The expenditures by the CCC on the dairy price support program vary to a considerable extent. The recent low in dollar expenditures was $68.6 million in 1965–1966; the recent high was $496.1 million in 1974–1975.[46] Table 2-4 summarizes activity under the price support program since 1960. The net removal of dairy products by the CCC as a milk equivalent percentage of total production also varies widely. Less than 1 percent was removed in 1973–1974, while nearly 9 percent was removed in 1961–1962.[47] The figure generally ranges in the vicinity of 2 percent to 5 percent. The price support program is expensive, and Congress had hoped to discourage overproduction of milk by enacting "base plan" legislation in 1965,[48] but such supply control attempts have neither been widely used nor proven effective.[49]

Import Quotas. The federal milk market order program is also supplemented by import quota restrictions. The Agricultural Adjustment Act authorizes the President to recommend to the International Trade Commission that an investigation be undertaken to determine whether or not "any article or articles are being or are practically certain to be imported into the United States under such conditions and in such quantities as to render or tend to render ineffective, or materially interfere with, any program or operation undertaken under this chapter."[50] The President so acts whenever the secretary of agriculture has reason to believe that this may be the case and makes such a recommendation to the President. If the secretary of agriculture

---

[44] 7 U.S.C., section 1301(a)(1).

[45] U.S. Department of Agriculture, *Agricultural Statistics 1973*, p. 457; *Agricultural Statistics 1975*, p. 451.

[46] U.S. Department of Agriculture, Agricultural Stabilization and Conservation Service, *A.S.C.S. Commodity Fact Sheet* (June 1975), p. 3. The figure for 1974–1975 was provided by ASCS personnel from data sheets available in their office.

[47] Ibid.

[48] U.S. Congress, Senate, Committee on Agriculture and Forestry, *Explanation of the Food and Agriculture Act of 1965*, Committee Print, 89th Congress, 1st session, October 12, 1965, p. 11.

[49] See Table 3–4 below and the accompanying discussion in the text.

[50] 7 U.S.C., section 624.

Table 2-4
SUMMARY OF MILK PRICE SUPPORT PROGRAM, 1960–1975

Year[a]	Total Milk Production (billions of pounds)	Net Removals (billions of pounds)	Percent Removed	Net CCC Expenditures[b] (millions of dollars)
1975	115.5	2.4	2.08	496.1
1974	114.8	0.7	0.61	70.9
1973	119.0	5.0	4.20	152.8
1972	119.3	6.6	5.53	338.2
1971	117.4	7.1	6.05	421.8
1970	116.2	4.4	3.79	290.9
1969	116.6	4.8	4.12	327.3
1968	118.2	7.0	5.92	364.2
1967	119.8	2.7	2.25	317.4
1966	122.2	2.9	2.37	68.6
1965	126.9	8.2	6.46	333.7
1964	126.2	7.5	5.94	379.1
1963	125.8	8.8	7.00	485.5
1962	126.3	11.2	8.87	612.0
1961	123.2	3.3	2.68	281.3
1960	122.7	3.4	2.77	218.2

a Market year, April 1–March 31.

b Fiscal year, July 1–June 30. Net expenditures include expenditures on the price support program and related programs minus CCC sales for unrestricted use.

Source: Data provided by U.S. Department of Agriculture, Agricultural Stabilization and Conservation Service.

determines that any emergency exists, the President may take immediate action. Thus, the import quota serves a function similar to that of the CCC support program in that the M-W price can be raised by excluding products that would compete with domestically produced dairy products. As of 1975, import quotas applied to such commodities as butter, dried milk products, condensed milk, and cheeses of various types.[51] The United States has generally been a net exporter of dairy products.[52]

[51] U.S. Department of Agriculture, The Impact of Dairy Imports on the U.S. Dairy Industry, A Report for the Senate Committee on Agriculture and Forestry, pp. 58–59.

[52] U.S. Department of Agriculture, 1975 Handbook of Agricultural Charts, Agricultural Handbook No. 491 (October 1975), p. 98.

State Regulation. Finally, milk is subject to extensive state regulation, in some cases overlapping federal regulation. As of January 1972, thirty-seven states and Puerto Rico had some form of milk regulation. The most common provisions establish prices at the producer level, the wholesale level, or the retail level. Nineteen states established minimum prices of some sort as of 1972. States also frequently regulate trade practices. It is common for sales below cost, price discrimination, discounts, and rebates to be regulated at both the wholesale and the retail levels. Many states also authorize milk promotion activity funded through either producer or handler assessments or with public moneys.[53]

As nearly as can be determined, every state has either federal or state regulation of milk prices. California is the most significant production region not covered by federal milk orders. But the state government in California regulates milk prices in a manner similar to the federal system, utilizing the classified pricing mechanism.

Market Structure of the Dairy Industry

The dairy industry can be divided into distinct segments, each with its own characteristic market structure. These segments are: (1) the milk producers; (2) the handlers (processors), both fluid and manufacturing; (3) the retailers, especially grocery chains; and (4) producer cooperatives. These segments can overlap, especially where cooperatives or retailers are also handlers. The various segments will be examined separately.

Producers. The tendency in the milk industry is for more production to be supplied by fewer producers operating larger farms. Production levels have remained fairly constant, while productivity has increased dramatically. In 1950 more than 1 million farms reported milk sales, while in 1970 this figure was down to 360,000.[54] In 1973 more than 50 percent of total milk production was produced on farms with herds of more than fifty cows, while these farms represented only 15.5 percent of all farms reporting milk cows. As late as 1964, small herds (those with less than twenty head) produced 22.7 percent of the national milk supply. By 1973 they accounted for less than

---

[53] U.S. Department of Agriculture, Economic Research Service, *Governments' Role in Pricing Fluid Milk in the United States*, Agricultural Economic Report No. 229 (July 1972), p. 13.

[54] Tucker, *Need for Restructuring Dairy Cooperatives*, p. 13. The 1970 figure is for farms with sales of $2,500 and over.

7 percent.[55] The total number of dairy cows in the United States has been dropping constantly, while the average production per cow has been increasing dramatically; see Table 2-5. Total milk production has stayed fairly constant over the years. In 1930, approximately 100 billion pounds of milk were produced. Production peaked during the early 1960s at approximately 125 billion pounds and is currently in the vicinity of 115 billion pounds.[56]

The value of farm investment is also going up rapidly. The 1969 Census of Agriculture reveals that the value of land and buildings has increased 217 percent on a per-acre basis since the 1950 Census of Agriculture was taken. The value of dairy farms increased dramatically between 1964, when the per-acre value was $189.94, and 1969, when the per-acre value was $274.39, an increase of 44 percent. That compares with an increase of 39 percent for farmland in general.[57]

The 1969 Census of Agriculture also revealed that 27.6 percent of the dairy acreage was operated by a lessee.[58] This statistic is of particular importance when considering the incidence of the benefits which may result from regulation of milk prices. More than one-fourth of dairy acreage is rented land. A lessee will be able to earn only a competitive wage for his labor; the cost of the lease would reflect the capitalized value of higher prices for milk that may result. The benefits of the capitalized value of higher prices accrue to the landowner. Ninety percent of leased dairy acreage is rented from nonfarmer landlords,[59] a group which it is unlikely the regulation was intended to benefit.

The percentage of milk producers belonging to dairy cooperatives is increasing. In 1960, about 80 percent of the producers delivering to federal milk order markets were cooperative members;[60] by 1970, more than 86 percent of the milk was delivered by coopera-

---

[55] U.S. Department of Agriculture, *The Impact of Dairy Imports on the U.S. Dairy Industry*, A Report for the Senate Committee on Agriculture and Forestry, pp. 8–9.

[56] U.S. Department of Agriculture, *Agricultural Statistics 1975*, p. 364.

[57] U.S. Department of Commerce, *1969 Census of Agriculture*, vol. 2, *General Report*, p. 33. Comparable data for previous years appears in earlier censuses, which are taken every five years. The 1974 census was not available when this study was being prepared.

[58] Ibid.

[59] Ibid.

[60] Donald R. Davidson, *Impact of Dairy Cooperatives on Federal Order Milk Markets*, U.S. Department of Agriculture, Farmer Cooperative Service, General Report No. 114 (August 1963), p. 17.

Table 2-5

AVERAGE MILK PRODUCTION PER COW IN THE
UNITED STATES, 1930 AND 1974

Year	Number of Dairy Cows	Total Milk Production (millions of pounds)	Average Production per Cow (pounds)
1930[a]	22,218	100,158	4,508
1974[b]	11,221	115,416	10,286

[a] George C. Tucker, *Need for Restructuring Dairy Cooperatives*, U.S. Department of Agriculture, Farmer Cooperative Service, USDA Service Report 125 (July 1972), p. 15.
[b] U.S. Department of Agriculture, *Agricultural Statistics 1975* (1975), p. 364.

tive members.[61] In addition, the number of cooperatives is decreasing, while the average size of cooperatives is increasing.

Handlers. Like the production of raw milk on the farms, the processing of milk has also become more concentrated, both in fluid bottling and in other manufacturing. According to the Census of Manufacturers, the number of fluid milk bottlers declined from 5,828 in 1958 to 3,481 in 1967.[62] As might be expected with a decreasing number of establishments, the average concentration ratios in local markets have been increasing. The concentration ratios for fluid milk bottling are based on the sales by the four largest firms in a federal milk order as a percentage of the total sales in the order. The average concentration ratios for four-firm sales in federal milk order areas went from 60 percent in 1953 to 66 percent in 1965.[63] Because packaged fluid milk products can easily be shipped 250 miles without spoilage problems, the notion that a federal market order area coincides with the true geographic market has been questioned. Accordingly, when the fluid sales market was taken to include all processing plants within a 250-mile radius of a central city, whether such plants actually made sales in the city or not, a significantly lower concentration resulted. In 1965 the figure was 41.7 percent,[64] as compared to the

[61] Milk Pricing Advisory Committee, *The Milk Pricing Problem*, Report to the U.S. Department of Agriculture, Part I (March 1972), p. 32.
[62] Tucker, *Need for Restructuring Dairy Cooperatives*, p. 28.
[63] Parker, *Staff Report to the Federal Trade Commission*, p. 46.
[64] Ibid.

66 percent referred to above. The concentration ratios in smaller markets are considerably higher than those in the larger markets. The four-firm figure for markets of less than 8 million pounds was 70 percent in 1962, while in markets with more than 60 million pounds of sales volume the four-firm figure was 48 percent.[65] Nonetheless, it does *not* appear that fluid milk processors recently have been able to exercise a great deal of market power. They often face dominant cooperatives in their buying market,[66] and large buyers in their selling market. The 1973 report of the Federal Trade Commission on the dairy industry concluded that, although the buyers and sellers of bottled fluid milk are both highly concentrated, the recent balance of power has shifted in favor of buyers.[67] The report cited excess capacity, consumer acceptance of private labels, and increased buying by chain stores as reasons. Data on the profitability of fluid milk processors further indicate that high market shares have not been translated into higher profits.

Concentration in the manufacturing milk industry is also increasing but, because the market for these less perishable dairy products is national in character, the number of participants is still large. In 1944 there were 9,739 processing plants. By 1970 this figure was 3,724. Over that same time period, average output per plant increased from 5.6 million pounds to 16.2 million pounds.[68] In the period 1961 to 1972, the total number of manufacturing plants dropped 46 percent, while the average output per plant rose 81 percent.[69]

Producer cooperatives are becoming increasingly involved in raw milk manufacturing. In 1970 and 1971 the number of dairy company acquisitions made by cooperatives exceeded the number made by non-cooperatives, reversing the historic patterns.[70] A recent study of producer cooperatives in the North Central region of the country revealed that approximately one-third of the milk marketed by cooperatives in that region was processed in their own facilities. Of the milk processed by the cooperatives, more than 86 percent was manufactured into nonfluid (and hence less perishable) products. In general,

---

[65] Ibid., p. 50.

[66] Although the raw milk that processors buy can, as a technological matter, be shipped great distances, federal milk orders discourage interorder shipments. Therefore, the geographic market in which the processor can reasonably buy is greatly diminished.

[67] Parker, *Staff Report to the Federal Trade Commission*, p. 7.

[68] Tucker, *Need for Restructuring Dairy Cooperatives*, p. 27.

[69] U.S. Department of Agriculture, *The Impact of Dairy Imports on the U.S. Dairy Industry*, A Report for the Senate Committee on Agriculture and Forestry, p. 11.

[70] Parker, *Staff Report to the Federal Trade Commission*, p. 14.

the larger cooperatives manufactured more of their milk in nonfluid products on a percentage basis than did the smaller cooperatives.[71]

Retailers. The trend in recent years has been for large retail grocery chains to be more significant participants in the processing of milk products. In 1971 an average of 27 percent of all milk was processed in vertically integrated plants in thirty-nine metropolitan areas of more than 1 million population. The FTC report identifies 1960 as the year when the trend of grocery chains integrating into milk processing began. This trend has continued. The trend was considered to have such an impact on the performance of the dairy industry that an entire chapter of the FTC report is devoted to vertical integration by grocery chains. Forward integration by producer cooperatives is also discussed. The report concludes that the threat of integration by food chains has a desirable price effect and has the structural effect of reducing concentration among independent processors because the larger processors were more often the former suppliers of the integrated chain. The most serious anticompetitive effect foreseen by the report is the reduced entry by and possible elimination of independent processors who are caught between backward integration by chains and forward integration by cooperatives.[72]

Producer Cooperatives. Changes in the role of producer cooperatives in the marketing of milk have been occurring as quickly as changes in the character of the other market participants. The number of producer cooperatives has been steadily declining, while their net sales have consistently shown increases. Between 1950 and 1970 the number of cooperatives dropped 50 percent but the net sales volume increased 165 percent.[73] In 1960 the number of producers delivering to federal milk market order regions who belonged to cooperatives was 80 percent.[74] By 1970 this figure was 86.5 percent,[75] and in 1974 it had grown to 87.9 percent.[76] In December 1973 more than 99 percent

---

[71] R.E. Deiter, J.W. Gruebele, and E.M. Babb, "Services Provided by Dairy Cooperatives and What Do They Cost" (Preliminary paper presented at Mid-West Milk Marketing Conference, Columbus, Ohio, March 23–24, 1976), Tables 3 and 4.

[72] Parker, *Staff Report to the Federal Trade Commission*, pp. 100–17.

[73] U.S. Department of Agriculture, Farmer Cooperative Service, *Cooperative Growth*, FCS Information 80 (March 1973), p. 34.

[74] Davidson, *Impact of Dairy Cooperatives on Federal Order Milk Markets*, p. 17.

[75] Milk Pricing Advisory Committee, *The Milk Pricing Problem*, Part I, p. 32.

[76] Robert W. March, deputy director, Dairy Division, Agricultural Marketing Service, U.S. Department of Agriculture, Memorandum to all market administrators re: Cooperatives in Federal Milk Order Markets (August 19, 1975), p. 1.

of the milk delivered in twenty-five of the sixty-one federal market orders was delivered by members of cooperative associations. In forty-six markets the percentage of producers belonging to cooperatives exceeded 90 percent.[77]

Control of producer cooperatives is generally vested in a board of directors, similar to that of a corporation. The size of the board may vary from a small number to thirty or more. Directors are generally farmers themselves, although management of the cooperatives is often handled by professionals. The board of directors is responsible to the membership. If the cooperative pays dividends on stock or membership capital in excess of 8 percent per year, the Capper-Volstead Act requires that votes be on a one member–one vote basis.[78] In matters affecting federal market order regulation, producer cooperatives are empowered to bloc vote for their members.[79] Therefore, the board of directors, and in some instances the manager, can vote for the entire membership in federal market order referenda. Since 1973 nearly all the votes cast in federal milk order referenda have been cooperative bloc votes.[80]

Producer cooperatives are increasingly assuming the roles of providers of services, both to producer-members and to the milk market as a whole. Among the services most frequently provided to the producer are: checking weights and tests, field services, inspections, guaranteeing a daily market outlet, selling supplies and equipment, providing insurance programs, and providing marketing information. Services provided on a market-wide basis often include advertising, public relations, and similar efforts. An increasingly widespread function of the producer cooperative is the "handling of surplus milk," also called "balancing supplies." In order to guarantee a market for excess milk produced by the members, cooperatives often undertake to process the surplus into manufactured products themselves,[81] often at a reported loss. In 1973–1974, 49 percent of all dairy cooperatives operated either fluid processing or manufacturing plants.[82] This function is often claimed to be a service to the market.

---

[77] U.S. Department of Agriculture, "Percentage of Producers Belonging to Cooperative Associations" (December 1973).

[78] 7 U.S.C., section 291.

[79] Ibid., section 608c(12).

[80] U.S. Department of Agriculture, Agricultural Marketing Service, Dairy Division, an attachment to a letter from Robert W. March to Vicki C. Golden, attorney, U.S. Department of Justice, March 19, 1976.

[81] Deiter, Gruebele, and Babb, "Services Provided by Dairy Cooperatives and What Do They Cost," Table 7.

[82] Data compiled by George Tucker, Farmer Cooperative Service, U.S. Department of Agriculture, for Janet Hall, U.S. Department of Justice, letter of May 27, 1976.

Merger activity has long been characteristic of producer cooperatives. During the 1950s and early 1960s, single-market mergers predominated.[83] Since 1967, however, there have been significant regional mergers. Among these are the progressive mergers of numerous local cooperatives that resulted in Associated Milk Producers, Inc. (AMPI); Mid-America Dairymen, Inc. (Mid-Am); and Dairymen, Inc. (DI). AMPI, formed in 1969, is located primarily in the South Central region of the country and in Indiana, Illinois, and Wisconsin. AMPI sold 10.8 billion pounds of milk in 1970.[84] Volume in fiscal 1973 was 14.9 billion pounds.[85] Mid-Am was formed in 1968, operates primarily in the West North Central portion of the country, and had an annual volume of 7.5 billion pounds in 1970.[86] DI, also formed in 1968, operates in the Southeast and sold 5.2 billion pounds in 1970.[87] These three cooperatives sold 20 percent of all milk produced in the United States in 1970.

Although concentration of producer cooperatives on the national level is not extremely high, concentration in individual federal market orders is. Table 2-6 reveals that at the end of 1973 thirty of sixty-one federal orders had one cooperative with more than 75 percent of the producers in the order.

Also in line with this trend are the formation of various "bargaining federations" throughout the country. "Bargaining federation" is loosely defined as a cooperative of cooperatives which acts as a central bargaining agent for milk sold to handlers by the member cooperatives. The large regional cooperatives are often members of regional federations. To the extent that federations operate in federal order markets, Table 2-6 well understates concentration. As of 1970, the more significant federations included Associated Dairymen, Inc., organized in 1964 and representing 53,000 producers marketing 20 billion pounds of milk a year. Associated Dairymen has since disintegrated following the formation of AMPI but had operated in the entire central portion of the country from Texas through Minnesota and Wisconsin. Great Lakes-Southern Milk, Inc., was organized in

---

[83] Ronald D. Knutson, *Cooperative Bargaining Developments in the Dairy Industry, 1960–1970*, U.S. Department of Agriculture, Farmer Cooperative Service, FCS Research Report No. 19 (August 1971), p. 10.

[84] Ibid., pp. 10–11.

[85] Philip Eisenstadt, Robert T. Masson, and David Roddy, *An Economic Analysis of the Associated Milk Producers, Inc., Monopoly*, filed with the Court in United States v. Associated Milk Producers, Inc., 394 F. Supp. 29 (W.D. Mo. 1975), affirmed, 534 F.2d 113 (8th Cir. 1976), p. 183.

[86] Knutson, *Cooperative Bargaining Developments in the Dairy Industry, 1960–1970*, pp. 10–11.

[87] Ibid.

Table 2-6

PERCENTAGE OF MILK PRODUCERS BELONGING TO THE
DOMINANT COOPERATIVE IN 61 FEDERAL ORDER MARKETS,
DECEMBER 1973

Percent	Number of Orders	Cumulative Total	Cumulative Percent
More than 99	13	13	21
90–99	5	18	30
75–90	12	30	49
60–75	13	43	70
45–60	9	52	85
Less than 45	9	61	100

Source: U.S. Department of Agriculture, Agricultural Marketing Service, Dairy Division.

1960 and represented 34,000 producers marketing 13.2 billion pounds of milk in 1970. Great Lakes operates through the entire southeastern portion of the country ranging up into Ohio and Michigan.[88] USDA is currently aware of sixteen major bargaining agencies.[89]

The preceding is a brief description of the market structure of dairy cooperatives today. Against this backdrop, the following section examines the behavior of dairy cooperatives in achieving this structure within the confines of regulation and the Capper-Volstead Act.

The Conduct of Dairy Cooperatives

As is evident from the legislative history, the Congress had certain limited purposes and goals in mind when it enacted the Capper-Volstead Act. Although there may be some dispute on the fine details of the act's goals, it is beyond dispute that the principal goal was to allow farmer groups the advantages equivalent to those afforded corporations so that the farmers would be able to fend for themselves in a marketplace theretofore dominated by the corporations with whom farmers dealt.

This goal has been achieved. Moreover, it has been exceeded, and to such an extent that problems unintended by Congress have

---

[88] Ibid., p. 7.

[89] Listing provided by Dairy Division, Agricultural Marketing Service, U.S. Department of Agriculture, and contained in a letter from Robert W. March, deputy director, to Roger Fones, U.S. Department of Justice, May 19, 1976.

been created by agricultural cooperatives in general and dairy co-operatives in particular. Congressional predictions that supply could not be controlled were offered in the 1920s to assuage the concern that cooperatives would abuse their exemption, achieve monopoly power, or charge a price in excess of a competitive price. Those predictions were, strictly speaking, correct. In 1922, however, Congress was unaware that cooperatives would one day operate in the federal order system, where market power is not the ability to control production, but rather the ability to control supply allocation between markets.[90]

Obtaining Market Power. This section will review the steps taken by cooperatives over the past ten to fifteen years to achieve market power.

Mergers. Mergers among dairy cooperatives have brought startling change to the cooperative scene. As noted by the Milk Pricing Advisory Committee, the merger of dairy cooperatives has initially concentrated in the southern markets, where the Class I utilization rate is high.[91] Producers in these markets had much to gain from achieving market power: to the extent a cooperative controls a southern market, the benefits of the higher ratio of Class I sales would flow to it alone. These large southern cooperatives soon recognized the attractiveness of their market and recognized that they had to control the flow of northern surplus milk into their orders. As a result, mergers spread northward.[92]

The exact history of the growth of each dominant cooperative in each order is not known. It is quite clear, however, that the position of a dominant cooperative has often been achieved through merger and consolidation. A study of selected midwestern markets showed a total of sixty-seven cooperatives in 1955. By 1965, of the twenty-nine cooperatives that had ceased to operate, twenty-five had merged or were consolidated with other cooperatives. Only one new cooperative was formed by a method other than consolidation.[93]

---

[90] This section is descriptive only of the ways market power is obtained. A more detailed discussion of what it is and how it is exercised is contained in chapter 4.

[91] Milk Pricing Advisory Committee, *The Milk Pricing Problem*, Part I, p. 30.

[92] Ibid. Other methods were also used to stop the flow of northern milk southward, such as the standby pool or full-supply contracts.

[93] S.N. Williams et al., *Organization and Competition in the Midwest Dairy Industries* (Ames, Iowa: Iowa State University Press, 1970), p. 65.

This information indicates that the concentration of market share in fewer cooperatives occurred primarily through merger.[94]

A review of the growth and development of the nation's four largest cooperatives will underline the role that mergers have played in the consolidation of market shares.[95] From 1968 until 1972, some 217 local cooperatives had merged into four regional cooperatives: AMPI; Dairymen, Inc.; Mid-America Dairymen; and Milk, Inc.[96] AMPI was incorporated on October 1, 1969. Its major predecessors were Pure Milk Association and Milk Producers, Inc. (MPI). MPI had been formed in 1967 through the consolidation of six cooperatives in Kansas, Oklahoma, Texas, and Arkansas.[97] After its formation, MPI undertook an active merger campaign.[98] Evidence of this conduct is reflected in MPI's growth: in 1967, it had 6,000 members; by April 1969, it had 8,000 members.[99] Since its formation, AMPI has acquired a large federated cooperative as a wholly owned subsidiary, as well as numerous local cooperatives.[100] By 1971, AMPI controlled more than 90 percent of the milk supply in eleven order markets and more than 70 percent in fourteen order markets.[101]

Mid-America Dairymen, Inc. (Mid-Am), was formed in 1968 through a series of mergers of thirty-one cooperatives serving Iowa, Kansas, Missouri, and Illinois.[102] In an article addressing the "latest surge toward consolidation of their cooperatives by dairy farmers," George Tucker of the Farmer Cooperative Service outlined the "series of mergers and consolidations that, in a little more than a year, reduced the number of organizations from 11 to 5 before the formation

---

[94] In fact, this evidence may underestimate the importance of merger activity in cooperatives achieving substantial market shares. As the Milk Pricing Advisory Committee reported, substantial concentration through merger occurred in the southern markets before spreading northward. Milk Pricing Advisory Committee, *The Milk Pricing Problem*, Part I, p. 30.

[95] It should not be overlooked that the nation's largest cooperatives control dominant shares in more than one market.

[96] Milk Pricing Advisory Committee, *The Milk Pricing Problem*, Part I, p. 30.

[97] Eisenstadt et al., *An Economic Analysis of the Associated Milk Producers, Inc., Monopoly*, p. 172.

[98] Knutson, *Cooperative Bargaining Developments in the Dairy Industry, 1960–1970*, p. 12.

[99] Eisenstadt et al., *An Economic Analysis of the Associated Milk Producers, Inc., Monopoly*, p. 174.

[100] Knutson, *Cooperative Bargaining Developments in the Dairy Industry, 1960–1970*, p. 12.

[101] Eisenstadt et al., *An Economic Analysis of the Associated Milk Producers, Inc., Monopoly*, p. 174.

[102] Knutson, *Cooperative Bargaining Developments in the Dairy Industry, 1960–1970*, p. 12.

of Mid-Am."[103]   In July 1967 three cooperatives in the Kansas City market had consolidated their operations into a new cooperative called Mid-America Dairymen, Inc. (This organization was different from the Mid-Am organization formed in 1968.) The first Mid-Am extended its operations in early 1968 with the purchase of a creamery. At the same time, Producers Creamery Company (PCC) of Springfield, Missouri, completed mergers with several cooperatives. Previously, PCC had formed a federation with two other dairy cooperatives, known as SLOMA. As Tucker reports:

> While SLOMA proved helpful to the three member cooperatives, they soon began studying the feasibility of a merger or consolidation. This resulting agreement to consolidate was expanded to include the first Mid-America Dairymen, Inc. . . . and Producers Creamery Company. . . . This consolidation completed the series that created the present Mid-America Dairymen, Inc.[104]

Dairymen, Inc., the principal dairy cooperative force in the Southeast, was originally formed by consolidation of eight cooperatives. In its first three years of operation, it had combined with sixteen additional cooperatives. Milk, Inc., was formed in 1969 through consolidation of four cooperatives serving Ohio and Pittsburgh markets.[105] This pattern of mergers has led to substantial concentration in individual federal order markets.

Market share alone does not reveal the role the dominant cooperative plays in an order market. In some markets no cooperative will hold a dominant market share, but the market would still be controlled through collective activity with other cooperatives in the market. The Milk Pricing Advisory Committee noted factors in addition to market share that should be considered in determining a cooperative's control of a market: proximity to other (not controlled) sources of milk, contract arrangements, and the extent of market coordination and other intercooperative activity.[106]

However, a single cooperative achieving a dominant share of any one market, as revealed in Table 2-6, is the key element for market power in a federal order market.[107] In December 1970, in nine of the

---

[103] George Tucker, "New Dairy Co-op Serves Farmers in Mid-America," *News for Farmer Cooperatives*, September 1968, p. 12.

[104] Ibid.

[105] Knutson, *Cooperative Bargaining Developments in the Dairy Industry, 1960–1970*, p. 12.

[106] Milk Pricing Advisory Committee, *The Milk Pricing Problem*, Part I, p. 31.

[107] It should be remembered that one cooperative may be the dominant cooperative in more than one market.

sixty-two federal orders, 100 percent of *all* producers serving the market belonged to *one* cooperative. In more than half (thirty-two) of the orders, 80 percent or more of the producers in the order market belonged to *one* cooperative.[108] The situation was essentially the same in December 1973 when more than half (thirty-one) of the sixty-one orders were controlled by one cooperative which represented 74 percent or more of the producers in the order market.[109] If the mergers and consolidations that occurred in the 1960s and early 1970s had been challenged, it is unlikely that so few cooperatives, with so large a share of their markets, would have resulted.

Federations and marketing agencies in common. Cooperatives with farmer members have in turn formed organizations with other farmer cooperatives to further their mutual goals. These organizations—often a cooperative of cooperatives, or a marketing agency, or a federation of cooperatives—are all commonly referred to as federations. Federation activity has been vitally important in the growth of the large, regional cooperatives and in their efforts to realize the benefits of their individual market positions. Federation activity in the early 1960s allowed cooperative members the opportunity to observe firsthand the benefits of coordinated activity,[110] and this activity likely provided a forum in which merger or consolidation possibilities could be discussed. Subsequent to the formation of the large regional cooperatives in the late 1960s, federation activity became important again. It provided a means by which the now enlarged cooperatives could coordinate intermarket activities, while reaping the benefits of local market control.

Over the past ten years, there have been a variety of federations, some of which have disbanded, others of which continue to today. Federation activity can be limited merely to monitoring and participating in federal order hearings on behalf of its member cooperatives: no milk marketing is done through the federation. However, the federations which have had the greatest impact on milk marketing have coordinated the individual cooperative's milk marketing and, in some cases, have become the bargaining agent for members' milk.

It was mentioned above that market share was not the sole determinative factor in concluding that a cooperative had market power. Absent a dominant cooperative with a substantial market share, co-

---

[108] Milk Pricing Advisory Committee, *The Milk Pricing Problem*, Part I, p. 33.

[109] U.S. Department of Agriculture, "Percentage of Producers Belonging to Cooperative Associations."

[110] Knutson, *Cooperative Bargaining Developments in the Dairy Industry, 1960–1970*, p. 12.

operatives could still wield market power through a federation of cooperatives marketing in the order. Chicago is just such an order. A substantial amount of milk is pooled on the Chicago order,[111] in part because of its proximity to the northern milkshed. No one cooperative has a dominant market share by itself. However, one of AMPI's predecessors, Pure Milk Association, and other leading cooperatives in the Chicago area formed Central Milk Producer Cooperative (CMPC). In 1968 CMPC represented "90–95 percent of the milk on the Chicago market" and acted as a "bargaining, marketing, and pooling agency" for the cooperative members.[112] CMPC, as bargaining and sales agent for the Chicago cooperatives, has been successful in extracting prices substantially in excess of the order price from handlers,[113] *even though* the Chicago order is adjacent to the largest concentration of surplus milk in the nation.

As the Milk Pricing Advisory Committee noted, proximity to other, not controlled, sources of milk can lessen a cooperative's or a federation's control of a market. That CMPC was able to extract premiums successfully is explained in part by the fact that CMPC is a federation of approximately 90 percent of all area producers. However, particularly in light of the potentially constraining influences of proximate surpluses, this alone would be insufficient without some additional supply control, which will be discussed subsequently.

Great Lakes-Southern is a federation of cooperatives operating in many different orders, stretching at one time from the Canadian border to the Gulf of Mexico, and from the East Coast to the Mississippi River. In 1969 Great Lakes-Southern represented approximately 70 percent of the grade A milk produced in its area of membership, an area that encompassed 11.3 percent of total U.S. production.[114] Starting as early as 1966, the predecessor federation, Great Lakes Milk Marketing Federation, formed in 1960, began extracting premiums of 60 cents to 70 cents per hundredweight above the federal or state minimum prices in the orders where it operated.[115]

Federations outside the midwestern and southern regions have been important in their areas of operation as well. Penn-Marva Fed-

---

[111] Approximately 12 percent of all milk regulated by federal orders in 1975. U.S. Department of Agriculture, FMOMS, *Annual Summary for 1975*, Table 12.

[112] Williams et al., *Organization and Competition in the Midwest Dairy Industries*, p. 67.

[113] See, for example, "CMPC Price Announcement, April 1976," on file with the U.S. Department of Justice, Antitrust Division.

[114] Knutson, *Cooperative Bargaining Developments in the Dairy Industry, 1960–1970*, p. 5.

[115] Williams et al., *Organization and Competition in the Midwest Dairy Industries*, p. 67.

eration was formed in 1968 by the federation of Interstate Milk Producers, Maryland Cooperative Milk Producers, and Maryland-Virginia Milk Producers.

This Federation preceded the consolidation of the Delaware Valley, Upper Chesapeake, and Washington, D.C. federal orders. Prior to the merger of the three federal orders to form the Mid-Atlantic order, each of the three cooperatives was the major producer organization in its respective market.[116]

In 1973, Penn-Marva Federation represented about 60 percent of the producers in the then consolidated federal order.[117]

Five of the major producer organizations in the northeastern area are affiliated/federated with the New York-New England Dairy Cooperative Coordinating Committee (NY-NE DCCC). Included are: Dairylea Cooperative, Inc., the oldest cooperative in the area; Northeast Dairy Cooperative; Upstate Cooperative; Green Mountain Federation; and Yankee Milk, Inc. NY-NE DCCC represented, in 1973, approximately 60 percent of the producers in the North Atlantic States region.[118]

It is quite clear that several federations have been established for the purpose of consolidating the market position of the cooperative members to bargain better with handlers for higher prices. In connection with this goal, federations have succeeded in altering federal orders by presenting a "united front."[119] However, limitation of production has not been successfully achieved in the dairy industry. Because of the residual power in a dairy farmer to choose, individually, his own production level, and perhaps because the cooperatives recognized that much of their effort within the order system served only to call forth additional production as a normal market response, cooperatives turned from mere regional federations to a multiregional approach to control the movement of Class I eligible milk.

ARSPC standby pool. Although regional federation activity has been important in coordination of milk movement and marketing, a unique federated cooperative has been a key to effective cooperative

---

[116] J. Robert Strain et al., *The Associated Reserve Standby Pool Cooperative, Past Performance and Future Prospects,* Standby Pool Cooperative Study Committee (March 9, 1973), p. 63.

[117] Ibid.

[118] Ibid., pp. 63–64.

[119] Knutson, *Cooperative Bargaining Developments in the Dairy Industry, 1960–1970,* pp. 8–9.

control of individual federal order markets. This federation, the Associated Reserve Standby Pool Cooperative (ARSPC), has likely had the most significant impact on milk marketing, certainly in the midwestern and southern markets, since the order system was instituted. The origins of ARSPC date back to June 1964 when twenty-six fluid milk marketing cooperatives organized Associated Dairymen, Inc. (ADI).[120]

> Its purpose was to increase incomes of farmers supplying milk to federal order markets in those regions through improved bargaining, joint action in federal order hearings, and political action.[121]

However, in 1967 ADI developed a "highly significant standby pool."[122] ADI operated its standby pool until it was succeeded by ARSPC in May 1970. ARSPC was formed primarily by members of ADI and Great Lakes-Southern Federation.[123]

Without going into great detail about the actual operation of the standby pool federation, suffice it to say that it is a joint effort by cooperatives to control the amount of grade A milk available in the more southerly markets in which the participating cooperatives have a dominant market share. This is accomplished by sharing southern revenues with northern producers who are potential competitors. As such, it augments the market power that exists in those markets. Such an organization would be clearly vulnerable to antitrust attack were it not for the limited immunity afforded by the Capper-Volstead Act. Even so, the existence and operation of ARSPC has figured prominently in antitrust cases brought against some of its members.

Other tactics. As the Milk Pricing Advisory Committee suggested,[124] there are other indications to examine in addition to a cooperative's market share in determining if the cooperative has market power. As has been discussed, federation activity can substitute for a single dominant cooperative in control of a local market order. Further, proximity to alternative surplus supplies can affect the market power of even a dominant cooperative or federation in an order.[125] Of course, ARSPC successfully removed much of the ability of north-

---

[120] Williams et al., *Organization and Competition in the Midwest Dairy Industries*, p. 66.

[121] Ibid.

[122] Ibid.

[123] Eisenstadt et al., *An Economic Analysis of the Associated Milk Producers, Inc., Monopoly*, pp. 444 and 453.

[124] See text accompanying note 106 above.

[125] Milk Pricing Advisory Committee, *The Milk Pricing Problem*, Part I, p. 31.

ern surplus milk to weaken market power. In addition to federation activity and the standby pool, other tactics have been used by cooperatives to achieve or protect their control of a local or regional market.

1. Full-supply contracts: A method used to solidify the market power of a cooperative or federation in an order has been imposition of full-supply contracts. Although cooperatives often view full-supply contracts as a service to handlers,[126] it has been recognized that such contracts also provide a means of enabling a cooperative to extract over-order prices.[127] "The full-supply contract provides a strong basis for bargaining power where barriers to entry into a market are important."[128] Even if handlers accept the full-supply contracts because of benefits to them, such contracts effectively lock a handler into his supplier/cooperative, unless the handler can find an alternative source at one time for *all* his needs. When used in connection with tactics which eliminate alternative sources, such as the standby pool, full-supply contracts are a means of foreclosing an outlet for sales by a competing cooperative and, if used extensively, of foreclosing outlets for nonmember producers. Thus, the cooperative can increase its market share through the imposition of full-supply contracts. At one time, such contracts were used; the use of full-supply contracts now is apparently diminished.[129] However, its importance in securing market power in the late 1960s and early 1970s should not be overlooked.[130]

2. Vertical integration: Another method employed by cooperatives and federations to enhance their market power is the operation of processing plants, typically supply or manufacturing plants.[131] Cooperatives often explain the operation of these plants as a service to their members and to the order system: their argument is that only through cooperative processing plants is the surplus supply in each order efficiently managed. Without arguing the merits of this

---

[126] Report of the Interagency Task Force, *Price Impacts of Federal Market Order Programs*, pp. 10–11.

[127] Knutson, *Cooperative Bargaining Developments in the Dairy Industry, 1960–1970*, p. 19.

[128] Williams et al., *Organization and Competition in the Midwest Dairy Industries*, p. 77.

[129] See "Replies to Questionnaire Issued by the Antitrust Division, July 16, 1976, to 90 Selected Cooperatives," on file with the Antitrust Division, U.S. Department of Justice.

[130] See Eisenstadt et al., *An Economic Analysis of the Associated Milk Producers, Inc., Monopoly*, pp. 530 ff., for a discussion of the role full-supply contracts played when AMPI gained control of markets.

[131] Williams et al., *Organization and Competition in the Midwest Dairy Industries*, pp. 69–71.

position,[132] the fact remains that the cooperatives benefit from their role as handlers in federal orders. Although the actual processing or supply plant operations may be profitless, or operated at a loss, cooperative market power is enhanced by these operations in a market.[133] "Order handling by cooperatives . . . has, in many instances, enhanced the bargaining position of these associations."[134]

There are a number of reasons why cooperatives acquire plants. One is to convert the producers supplying that plant into cooperative members. An acquisition may be made because the acquired plant had been obtaining noncooperative milk at a price less than that offered by the cooperatives. Purchase of a proprietary plant may be done to eliminate a dealer who is price cutting, that is, selling his products at prices below those sold by dairies buying from the cooperative. A cooperative may acquire a plant to foreclose it as an outlet to nonmembers, to force them into the cooperative. Finally, a cooperative may acquire a plant to use it in "pool loading,"[135] or to price cut against proprietary handlers in an effort to force them to buy from the cooperative.[136]

Although vertical integration was foreseen as a likely outcome by the Congress when it enacted the Capper-Volstead Act, Congress did not contemplate that vertical integration would be used to obtain and extend control over a market by a cooperative.

Conclusion and Summary of Judicial Interpretation. Market power, in the form of control of the allocation of supply to markets, or control of the Class I eligible milk to a market, has been achieved by cooperatives today in the context of the order system. Through a pattern of consolidation by merger, intercooperative activity through federations, and other tactics, cooperatives over the last ten to fifteen

---

[132] Questions can be raised about the cause of the surplus, as well as the motivation to "handle" or control it.

[133] Williams et al., *Organization and Competition in the Midwest Dairy Industries*, p. 70.

[134] Davidson, *Impact of Dairy Cooperatives on Federal Order Milk Markets*, p. 23.

[135] "Pool loading" is a predatory practice without parallel outside of the dairy industry: it can only occur within the framework of the federal order system. In simple terms, pool loading is a conscious effort to lower the blend price in a market order region. This is accomplished by causing greater volumes of raw grade A milk to qualify as "producer milk" on the targeted order, thus qualifying it to receive the market blend price from the administrator of the order.

[136] USDA policy apparently treats a producer delivering to a cooperative-owned plant as a cooperative member, at least with respect to deliveries to that plant. Eisenstadt et al., *An Economic Analysis of the Associated Milk Producers, Inc., Monopoly*, pp. 565–81.

years have increased their market share and extended their control over alternative sources of milk to their markets.

The association of farmers into cooperatives is clearly not actionable under the Sherman Act. However, the courts have removed from the protection of the Capper-Volstead Act agreements with nonproducers. Further, it appears settled that the conspiracy provisions of section 1 of the Sherman Act apply to the predatory or anticompetitive conduct of a cooperative, and that section 2 of the Sherman Act is applicable to attempts to monopolize or monopolization. Although the existence of intercooperative associations are protected from the application of the Sherman Act, such associations' conduct is subject to scrutiny if it is not in the nature of "marketing."

The law with respect to mergers between cooperatives is not clear, although the generally accepted view has been that section 7 of the Clayton Act is not applicable to cooperative mergers. This view rests on several factors, including the allowance of marketing agencies in common which can be used to achieve market unity similar to a merger; the liberal thrust of congressional action toward cooperatives, including allowance of federations and exchange of marketing information; and the essential identity of mergers with the alternative, permitted approach of dissolution and reformation.

However, there is some reasoned support for the contrary conclusion, that section 7 is applicable to intercooperative mergers. This view deserves further exploration in terms of its legal and practical implications. It rests on the well-recognized principles of judicial interpretation of antitrust exemptions: such exemptions are not to be implied and, to the extent one is granted, it is to be interpreted narrowly. In light of these principles, there is at least room for a reasoned argument that intercooperative mergers should be subjected to scrutiny under section 7 of the Clayton Act. In addition, there are legal and economic factors that suggest that the difference between requiring cooperatives to dissolve and reform, as opposed to merge, may be more than a mere matter of form and has antitrust enforcement implications.

3

THE FEDERAL MILK ORDER SYSTEM CONTRASTED WITH AN UNREGULATED MARKET

This chapter examines the impact of the federal order system on the supply and marketing of raw milk. The analysis assumes that cooperatives, to the extent they exist, cannot alone possess market power great enough to influence price or affect supply. It is reasonable to believe that a similar assumption was made, at least implicitly, when Congress authorized the order system in the 1930s. At that time, producer cooperatives were numerous, usually small, local concerns just being organized. Now cooperatives are fewer in number, with some assuming significant roles in the marketplace. See Table 3-1. Granted that cooperative marketing of milk is more concentrated today, it is nonetheless worthwhile to evaluate the distortions created by the milk order system based on the notion that alone cooperatives do not exercise significant market power. This brings into focus the costs of the order system for the ultimate purpose of weighing them against the benefits attributable to regulation. (Studies estimating the dollar value of these costs are evaluated in chapter 5.)

The greatest impact of milk order provisions is on the supply of fluid grade milk. This is a result of the mechanism that milk orders use to set prices. This impact can be delineated as follows:

(1) Federal market orders create an overproduction of grade A milk because they set prices above an unregulated equilibrium level.

(2) Federal market orders reduce the amount of fluid milk consumed by raising the price of raw grade A milk used for fluid purposes.

(3) Federal market orders create an overproduction of manufactured dairy products produced from excess grade A milk.

Table 3-1

NUMBER OF DAIRY COOPERATIVES IN THE UNITED STATES, 1930–1970

	1930	1940	1950	1960	1970
Number of cooperatives	2,458	2,395	2,008	1,609	956

Source: George C. Tucker, *Need for Restructuring Dairy Cooperatives*, U.S. Department of Agriculture, Farmer Cooperative Service, USDA Service Report 125 (July 1972), p. 4.

(4) Federal market orders result in fluid milk consumers subsidizing the consumers of manufactured dairy products.

The federal orders also severely impede the mobility of raw fluid grade milk once it has been produced. Provisions of market orders discourage the transport of milk from areas of surplus productive capacity to areas of deficit supply.

A final effect of the order system, in conjunction with the price support program, is to elevate the general price level for dairy products, thus increasing the cost to consumers. It must be reemphasized that the deviations discussed here are deviations from an unregulated system. This is only half of the analysis. The other half is to examine whatever benefits may be derived from the government-induced deviations from an unregulated system. The ultimate goal must be to weigh the costs, measured as deviations from an unregulated system, against the benefits derived from governmental intervention in the milk market.

Provisions Affecting Supply

This section examines the provisions and terms of the federal order system insofar as it affects the supply of raw fluid milk. The section will treat classified pricing, the blend price mechanism, and Class I base plans.

Classified Pricing. Classified pricing is in effect in all federal market orders.[1] This is simply the practice of charging handlers two different prices for the same product, grade A milk, dependent solely on the end use made of that milk by the handler. Milk that is used in manufacturing is paid for at one price; milk that is processed for fluid use

---

[1] Classified pricing is authorized by 7 U.S.C., section 608c(5)(A).

is priced at a different (higher) rate. Fluid-use milk is called Class I; manufacturing-use milk is called Class II.

In an unregulated market, price differences based on use would disappear. All grade A milk would sell for a single price to fluid and manufacturing buyers alike. No producer would sell to a manufacturing handler at a price less than that being offered by fluid handlers, and artificially high prices for fluid-use handlers could not be maintained without enforcement mechanisms as competitive pressures would drive the price down to a free-market level.

Any price discrimination program must be enforced. Prior to market orders, producer cooperatives sometimes attempted to institute price discrimination on their own, largely unsuccessfully. It is unrealistic to expect handlers voluntarily to keep truthful and accurate records for the purpose of determining their end use of raw milk. Furthermore, to maintain effective classified pricing, the seller must be able to keep his buyers apart. If the buyers are able to deal with each other, Class II buyers can resell to Class I buyers to the benefit of both. Under federal market orders, it is the government that steps in to enforce the classified pricing system. Federal orders require handlers to file monthly reports to the "market administrator" (a USDA official responsible for overseeing one or more federal orders) and subject themselves to audits.

In the absence of enforcement by the government, the prices handlers pay for grade A milk, regardless of the use, would gravitate toward a level between the Class I and the Class II prices we now observe. This would result because Class I prices as currently set exceed Class II prices by more than the difference in cost involved in producing grade A milk instead of grade B.[2] In an unregulated market, grade A milk would still sell for more than grade B, but only by an amount sufficient to reflect the difference in cost.[3] With lower prices prevailing for grade A milk, more will be demanded for fluid-use purposes. The more grade A milk going into fluid use, the less there is to compete with grade B milk for manufacturing uses. With less grade A milk competing with it, the price of grade B milk will

---

[2] The additional cost of conversion is estimated to be about 15 cents per hundredweight; the *smallest* difference in price between Class I and Class II milk in federal orders is $1.06 per hundredweight.

[3] This price difference would be on an annual average basis. The price for grade A milk would fluctuate seasonally with supply. In the spring, the price difference between grade A and grade B milk may well be less than the cost of conversion, approaching the grade B price, because some grade A milk would be going into manufacturing uses. In the fall, the price would rise, as most grade A milk would be needed for fluid use. Over the course of the year, the average price difference between A and B must cover the conversion costs.

rise somewhat.[4] The federal order Class II price is equivalent to the grade B price, as it is based on the M-W price. Therefore, in an unregulated market, grade B prices would be higher than the current Class II prices, and grade A prices would exceed grade B prices by approximately the additional costs involved. Grade A milk, however, would sell for less than the current Class I federal order prices.

Because Class I prices are higher than the unregulated price that would prevail for grade A milk, less milk is consumed in fluid form than would be the case without regulation. Therefore, federal market orders, through price discrimination, reduce the amount of fluid milk consumed by the public by increasing its cost.

Consumption patterns suggest that consumers are finding substitutes for fluid milk products. Per capita consumption of fluid milk and cream has dropped from 302 pounds in 1965 to 244 pounds in 1974. See Figure 3-1. Class I prices in federal milk orders were steadily increasing over these years. The largest increase in the difference between the yearly average M-W price and the yearly weighted-average Class I price occurred between 1966 and 1968, increasing 45 cents per hundredweight in that two-year period. See Table 3-2. The size of the fluid differential is indicative of how much fluid milk consumption will be discouraged by the milk orders. The greater the differential, the higher the Class I price and the lower the consumption.

The Blend Price Mechanism. The blend price mechanism is the other side of classified pricing,[5] and it exists in all federal order markets except Puget Sound and Georgia, which have order-wide Class I base plans.[6] Classified prices are what buyers pay; blend prices are what producers receive. The blend price is a weighted-average price reflecting the prices paid for all of the grade A milk sold to regulated handlers in the federal market order. Thus, all producers receive a portion of the higher Class I revenues, regardless of how their particular milk is used. Under such a system, where buyers

---

[4] Note that grade B producers would be better off *without* government regulation. The sharp decline in the number of grade B producers in recent years is largely because of federal regulation. Thus, federal regulation has operated to favor one group of dairy farmers over another. The disadvantaged farmers are located primarily in the Upper Midwest.

[5] The blend price mechanism is authorized by 7 U.S.C., section 608c(5)(B). The blend price formula is:

$$\frac{(\text{Class I volume})(\text{Class I price}) + (\text{Class II volume})(\text{Class II price})}{\text{total volume}}.$$

[6] Some orders have seasonal incentive base plans in effect instead of blend prices part of the year.

Figure 3-1

ANNUAL PER CAPITA CONSUMPTION OF FLUID MILK AND
CREAM, AND WEIGHTED-AVERAGE CLASS I PRICES PER
HUNDREDWEIGHT IN FEDERAL MILK ORDER MARKETS,
1965–1974

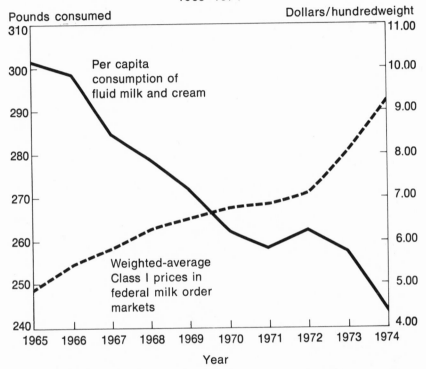

Source: U.S. Department of Agriculture, *Agricultural Statistics, 1975* (1975), p. 384; U.S. Department of Agriculture, Agricultural Marketing Service, *Federal Milk Order Market Statistics*, annual summaries, 1965–1974.

pay a price different from that which sellers receive, price does not play its customary function of bringing buyers and sellers together. This creates market distortions. In particular, purchasers of Class II milk pay less for it than the farmer receives for producing it, because the blend price exceeds the Class II price by definition. The producer is a price-taker who will make his output decision by equating his marginal cost of production with the blend price he receives. On the other hand, the marginal buyer, a Class II handler, only values this output at the Class II price, the price he pays for it. Thus, for the last units of milk produced, the cost of producing it exceeds the value

Table 3-2
WEIGHTED-AVERAGE FLUID DIFFERENTIALS IN FEDERAL MILK ORDER MARKETS, 1965–1975
(dollars per hundredweight)

Year	Weighted-Average Class I Price	Average M-W Price	Average Fluid Differential
1975	9.36	7.62	1.74
1974	9.35	7.06	2.29
1973	8.03	6.30	1.73
1972	7.10	5.08	2.02
1971	6.90	4.81	2.09
1970	6.74	4.66	2.08
1969	6.50	4.42	2.08
1968	6.23	4.17	2.06
1967	5.85	3.99	1.86
1966	5.53	3.92	1.61
1965	4.93	3.27	1.66

Source: U.S. Department of Agriculture, Agricultural Marketing Service, *Federal Milk Order Market Statistics*, annual summaries, 1965–1975.

placed on it by the buyer. The value placed on it by the buyer is a reflection of the value that society places on it. A misallocation of resources results, and it is reflected by the large surpluses of grade A milk that exist in most federal order markets. Thus, the federal order system is responsible for creating an unnecessary surplus of grade A milk supplies.

The degree of the surpluses can be measured by examining the "Class I utilization rates," also known simply as utilization rates, in federal order markets. For example, if a federal order has a utilization rate of 80 percent, this means that 80 percent of the milk sold to handlers regulated by that order was used for Class I purposes. It follows that 20 percent was used for Class II. The ratio of Class II milk to Class I milk is 20/80, or 25 percent. Therefore, such a market would have a surplus of grade A milk over and above Class I fluid needs of 25 percent.[7]

Table 3-3 gives annual and fall grade A surpluses in federal order markets on a market-wide basis since 1965. The table reveals

[7] For a map showing regional grade A surpluses in federal order markets in 1975, see U.S. Department of Agriculture, Agricultural Marketing Service, *Federal Milk Order Market Statistics, Annual Summary for 1975* (June 1976), pp. 44–45 (hereinafter cited as *FMOMS*). Many areas had well over twice as much grade A milk available as was actually used for fluid purposes.

Table 3-3

NATIONAL CLASS I UTILIZATION RATES AND
GRADE A SURPLUS IN FEDERAL ORDER MARKETS
FOR THE YEAR AND FOR THE SHORT SEASON, 1965–1975

(percent)

	Yearly Average		Short Season Surplus		
Year	Utilization	Surplus	September	October	November
1975	58	72	56	52	61
1974	58	72	64	54	54
1973	61	64	52	47	45
1972	60	67	52	52	47
1971	59	69	56	56	52
1970	62	61	52	47	52
1969	64	56	45	39	45
1968	65	54	45	37	37
1967	64	56	43	43	41
1966	66	52	39	41	41
1965	63	56	41	41	41

Source: U.S. Department of Agriculture, *Federal Milk Order Market Statistics*, annual summaries, 1965–1975.

a clear trend toward ever-increasing surpluses. The greater the surplus, the greater the misallocation of resources it indicates. The market-wide surplus in 1975 was 72 percent, indicating a very significant cost is involved. Grade A milk that cannot be sold at the established Class I price must be channeled into manufacturing uses. As noted above, grade A production is too high and fluid consumption is too low. Therefore, the amount of resources devoted to manufactured dairy products is necessarily too high. This trend has been increasing. The Class I utilization rate has dropped fairly consistently since the mid-1960s. Between 1965 and 1975 per capita grade A deliveries in federal order markets dropped 11.8 percent. However, per capita Class I utilization dropped 19.5 percent during that same period.[8] The increasing portion of grade A milk being diverted into manufacturing uses is to be expected because of the dual pricing in federal order markets.

With too much Class II production occurring in federal order markets, the final prices of manufactured dairy products to the consumer must be lower than would prevail in an unregulated market

---

[8] U.S. Department of Agriculture, *FMOMS*, annual summaries for 1965 and 1975.

in order for the Class II market to clear. Admittedly, the government plays a partial role in clearing the Class II market directly through the price support program, buying manufactured dairy products at preannounced prices. But this is only a partial solution. The rest of the market is cleared by artificially low prices for Class II products, the difference between Class II prices and the blend prices farmers receive being generated from Class I revenues. Therefore, under the classified/blend price system, fluid milk consumers subsidize manufactured dairy product consumers. This is true simply because Class II handlers are able to buy their raw Class II milk at a price below that which would exist in an unregulated market. As the lower costs are reflected in lower prices for manufactured dairy products, consumers will be demanding more of these products. The source of the subsidy for manufactured products is the prices paid by fluid milk product consumers. The higher Class I price set by the government is returned in part to all grade A producers, which in turn encourages their overproduction. This overproduction, paid for by the fluid milk consumers, results in surpluses which are then purchased by Class II handlers at less than the cost of producing the raw milk.

As noted above, the government must usually enter the dairy market at the buying end also, purchasing manufactured dairy products under the price support program administered by the Commodity Credit Corporation. The law does not permit the Class II price to fall all the way to a market clearing price if that price would be below the support level. Purchases must be made in order to assure that the M-W price is maintained at the support level. Thus, the government's role can be seen as one which in the first instance creates an overproduction of milk suitable for fluid use, and subsequently must purchase the manufactured products produced from the surplus. The government thereby assures an ultimate market for all milk produced by clearing it at a higher price.

Class I Base Plans. Most of the problems identified with the milk marketing system flow directly from the classified/blend price mechanism characteristic of federal order regulation. Even those who believe that class pricing is in the best interests of the dairy industry recognize the problems. Chief among these is the ever-increasing quantity of grade A milk being "pooled" (sold or accounted for) on federal orders to take advantage of the higher prices offered. New milk often comes from dairy farmers who convert grade B operations over to grade A farms.[9] This in turn creates the problem of trying

---

[9] Truman F. Graf and Robert E. Jacobson, *Resolving Grade B Conversion and Low Class I Utilization Pricing and Pooling Problems*, University of Wisconsin-

to channel the surplus efficiently into manufacturing uses. Efficiency is sought through regulations and performance standards rather than market forces. In addition, regulation of economic conduct inevitably injects equity as an issue among those regulated,[10] an issue not likely to be solved to everyone's satisfaction when the flow of product to market is legislated.

Side effects aside, the surplus problem remains. The fact that a surplus exists is largely by design. One goal of the market order system is to "insure a sufficient quantity of pure and wholesome milk" fit for fluid consumption is available.[11] Ironically, this availability is never translated into consumption. Instead, the very mechanism designed to create plenty of fluid milk has evolved into a system of reduced fluid consumption and oversupply of raw grade A milk. To date, efforts to control this problem have revolved, not around ending the classified pricing system, but around efforts to control production directly. Class I base plans represent one such effort.[12]

Market-wide Class I base plans are authorized by the statute.[13] A Class I base plan is an alternative to the blend price mechanism. Because these plans were perceived to involve production control, Congress apparently felt it was unwise to allow cooperatives to exercise this power. Accordingly, bloc voting in federal order hearings is prohibited on the issue of whether a base plan will be instituted.

Under orders with Class I base plans, each producer delivering to that order forms a "base" amount of milk depending on his marketings during a one-to-three-year period. Thereafter, each producer is paid a price similar to a Class I price on his deliveries up to the amount of his base. On all deliveries in excess of his base amount, he is paid a lower rate, similar to a Class II price.

In theory, paying producers under a Class I base plan instead of a blend price system would operate to eliminate the problem of the misallocation of resources which was described above. The producer

Madison, College of Agricultural and Life Sciences, Research Division, R2503 (June 1973), p. 3.

[10] Ibid., p. 13.

[11] 7 U.S.C., section 608c(18).

[12] Other forms of production control exist, but the thrust is similar to that of Class I base plans. "Seasonal incentive plans" are used in some orders, but usually they only apply during certain months of the year. For this reason they are claimed to be directed at "evening out" production. Also, some cooperatives administer their own private base plans which apply only to members. The observations made concerning Class I base plans are generally applicable to these other supply control plans.

[13] 7 U.S.C., section 608c(5)(B)(f).

would not receive a blend price for his marginal production; rather, he would receive only a Class II price for all milk delivered in excess of his base. Of course, a Class I base plan does nothing to alter the effects of classified pricing, that is, the amount of milk going into fluid use is still restricted because of the higher Class I price.

Class I base plans do not appear to work effectively in practice, however. To date, only two federal order markets have instituted Class I base plans, the Puget Sound order[14] and the Georgia order.[15] Although it is impossible to tell what would have happened had base plans not been in effect, a comparison of pre- and post-enactment production data suggests that the Class I base plans had no effect. See Table 3-4. Indeed, the surplus problem seems to be increasing in both orders. The Puget Sound base plan was instituted in September 1967 and revised in July 1971. In 1967 the market-wide Class I utilization rate was 48 percent. Although the utilization rate rose slightly in 1968 and 1969, it has declined steadily since then. In 1973 and in 1974 it was 39 percent; in 1975 it was 41 percent. In Georgia, the base plan was instituted in March of 1972. The Georgia order itself has only been in effect since April 1969 and to date no clear trend has developed. Utilization rates have been between 80 percent and 90 percent.

In addition to their questionable effectiveness, Class I base plans may also have some undesirable side effects. The most obvious is that there is erected a barrier to entry by producers who do not have bases. A producer is unlikely to enter the market if he will be receiving a Class II price for all or substantially all of his output. If new base can be formed by new entrants (or by established producers increasing output during the short season), new entry will occur, creating new base, and thus diluting the excess return generated by restricting supply under a base plan. Base is expandable under the federal order Class I base plans, although a time requirement establishes a partial entry barrier. If the amount of base were fixed, then monopoly rents would accrue to the original base holders.

Another possible side effect is the dumping of nonbase milk by producers in other markets. Instead of accepting a lower Class II price for part of his milk, a producer may find it profitable to sell his nonbase milk in another order, thereby receiving a blend price instead. This can even have the effect of actually increasing production since the producer could receive a Class I price on some milk and a blend price on the rest. This practice would generate more revenue for the producer than receiving a blend price for all deliveries, but it would

---

[14] 7 C.F.R., section 1125 and following (1976).
[15] Ibid., section 1007 and following (1976).

Table 3-4

CLASS I UTILIZATION RATES AND GRADE A SURPLUS IN
PUGET SOUND AND GEORGIA, 1964–1975

(percent)

Year	Georgia		Puget Sound	
	Utilization	Surplus	Utilization	Surplus
1975	41	144	82	22
1974	39	156	84	19
1973	39	156	90	11
1972[a]	41	144	86	16
1971	43	133	84	19
1970	47	113	82	22
1969[b]	52	92	88	14
1968	51	96		
1967[c]	48	108		
1966	46	117		
1965	44	127		
1964	45	122		

[a] Georgia Base Plan instituted March 1972.
[b] Georgia order instituted April 1, 1969.
[c] Puget Sound Base Plan enacted September 1967, revised July 1971.
Source: U.S. Department of Agriculture, *Federal Milk Order Market Statistics*, annual summaries, 1965–1975. Compiled from data contained therein.

magnify the overproduction problem that the base plan was designed to alleviate.

Provisions Affecting the Mobility of Raw Grade A Milk

In addition to affecting the supply of raw fluid milk as to quantity, the federal order system also affects supply in the sense that its provisions have a great impact upon the extent to which the existing supply moves from surplus areas to deficit areas of the country. One of the guiding philosophies of milk regulation is that local fluid markets should be supplied by local milk producers.[16] In the same vein, it is also considered desirable that local markets "handle their own sur-

[16] Milk Pricing Advisory Committee, *The Milk Pricing Problem*, Report to the U.S. Department of Agriculture, Part I (March 1972), p. 1. This notion is undergoing some rethinking and criticism. See Roland W. Bartlett, "Bringing Federal Order Class I Pricing Up to Date and in Line with Antitrust Regulations," *Illinois Agricultural Economics*, January 1974, p. 8.

plus," that is, excess production of grade A milk from local producers should be pooled locally. Effectively isolating local markets requires that incentives to ship milk between orders be minimized to the extent possible.

There are two general ways in which the transport of raw milk is restricted. The first method is simply control of marketing by regional cooperatives or bargaining federations, especially in the surplus producing regions of the Upper Midwest. The Associated Reserve Standby Pool Cooperative is also important in this regard. The second method, analyzed here, is through provisions of the federal market orders. The order system encourages local handlers to buy from local producers. Naturally, local producers wish to receive as high a price as possible for their milk without attracting milk from distant sources. One study refers to this problem faced by milk producers as one of "protect[ing] themselves from other source milk through pricing provisions."[17] In order to insulate local markets effectively, local producers must be protected from two types of competition. The first type is competition from other milk producers who would ship their milk into the local market. Such producers are referred to as "pool riders," indicating that they draw the blend price from the local market pool when their milk is not needed for local fluid needs and they are located outside of what could be considered the "normal" supply area for the market.

The second type is competition from milk that would be shipped into the market from handlers who have bought milk from producers in other areas and then reshipped into the local market. Protection from other producers is provided by the pricing system; protection from other handler shipments comes from the "allocation provisions" of federal market orders.

Local producers are protected from competition from distant producers because the price paid by a handler is the price that is regulated. Producers are regulated indirectly under an order only when and if they sell milk to a regulated handler. A regulated handler will pay an identical price for any producer milk he receives regardless of the source of that milk. Milk bought from a producer just down the road costs exactly the same as milk bought from a producer located across the country. As long as a handler is buying producer milk, he would naturally purchase it from a local producer so long as local producer milk is available. Such milk would always be fresher and more dependable. Of course, if monopoly premiums are being

---

[17] J. Robert Strain et al., *The Associated Reserve Standby Pool Cooperative: Past Performance and Future Prospects,* Standby Pool Cooperative Study Committee (March 9, 1973), p. 2.

charged by local cooperatives, then milk from more distant producers who are not members of the local cooperative becomes more attractive if the distant producer can undercut the premium.

In addition, incentives are built into the order pricing structure to encourage producers to sell locally. A producer located within any federal order region is encouraged to ship his milk towards the center of his own federal order market rather than away from that center. This is so because producers receive what are known as "zoned-out" blend prices for the milk they deliver to regulated handlers. The zone differentials depend on the zone in which the buyer is located.[18] The further the handler is from the population center of the order region, the less the price received by the producer.

As an example, assume that the area around the population center is called zone 1. A producer delivering to a handler in zone 1 receives the full blend price. As the distance that the handler is located from the center of the order increases, the actual blend price received by the delivering producer is reduced. Thus, the producer is responsible for the cost of transporting his milk to a handler. The zones are drawn similar to concentric circles from the market center. As long as the producer ships towards the market center, he will be receiving a higher price for his milk. The price difference as designed does not quite compensate the farmer for the added costs of shipping his milk. He receives a higher price only so long as he ships toward a higher priced zone. Therefore, a producer located in zone 3 will be compensated for the cost of shipping his milk only so long as he ships toward zone 1. Given price alignment he would generally not ship to his north, but rather towards a market center located generally to his south. Since the zone differentials do not fully compensate for actual transport costs, the closest southern market center is a preferred marketplace. Thus, all producers have an incentive to ship towards a single market center, and zone differentials have the characteristic of helping delineate localized markets.

The second, and more problematical, source of outside competition is milk received from distant handlers. At this point it should be noted that the prices of milk in federal order markets are "aligned" to reflect the costs of transporting milk between markets farther away from the Minnesota-Wisconsin area, which acts as a base point. Prices increase as one moves south.

Local handlers could conceivably purchase milk from either handlers regulated on another order or unregulated handlers. The situation that would frequently develop is one where a high fluid-use

---

[18] Zone differentials are authorized by 7 U.S.C., sections 608c(5)(A)3 and (B)(ii)(c).

handler in the local market will purchase surplus grade A milk from a manufacturing-use handler in another area. These sales are not subject to the classified pricing provisions, which apply only to milk bought from producers. These sales, however, are subject to "allocation provisions." The allocation provisions are accounting rules for determining which milk received from what sources by a handler will be placed in which use classes for purposes of calculating the handler's milk bill due to the local pool each month. Although some rules are needed if classified pricing is to be effective,[19] the allocation provisions are so designed as to aid in the insulation of local markets. Although the allocation provisions are complex, the overall effect is to create a presumption in favor of local milk as to which was used for fluid purposes; other milk is more likely to be assigned manufacturing classification. In this way, distant sources receive less of the benefit of local Class I prices. Under the allocation provisions, local producer milk is disproportionately "promoted" into Class I usage, while other purchases are treated predominately as Class II. To the extent that a handler is required to pay transport costs on Class II milk purchased from distant sources, it is not profitable for him to go elsewhere to purchase his milk.

A handler pays a greater total bill for all of his milk requirements if he purchases milk from handlers regulated on another order or from an unregulated handler than if he simply buys local producer milk. It must be constantly borne in mind, however, that this will *not* be the case where premiums are being charged by cooperatives in a handler's local market. If the local cooperative is charging substantial over-order prices, there is an incentive for the handler to seek distant sources of supply from handlers or producers operating in markets without over-order prices. When this is the case, the distant milk can be transported (particularly in a north-to-south direction) and sold for a price that undercuts the local premium. Of course, a small premium creates only a small incentive to overcome the local bias of the allocation provisions. It may be necessary for premiums to be more significant before handlers will justify the added trouble of seeking distant supplies.

Provisions Affecting Price Levels

So far, this chapter has examined terms and provisions of the federal order system and distortions they create on the raw fluid grade milk

---

[19] All milk received at a handler's plant is immediately intermingled with other raw milk supplies on hand, so that determining the actual use of any specific milk is impossible. Thus, the need exists for accounting rules.

markets. The greatest distortions are found to result primarily from the classified pricing and blend price mechanisms. Furthermore, there are collateral provisions which discourage milk movements between market areas.

The impact on prices will now be considered. The effects of the order system on price levels result in large part from the pricing relationships that are sought to be maintained among orders, in addition to the prices set in each individual order. Moreover, the interaction between the milk price support program and the order system affects price levels directly; that topic is also discussed in this section.

Base Point Price Alignment. As alluded to above, prices for milk in federal order markets are aligned using a base point in the milkshed, often taken as Eau Claire, Wisconsin,[20] and setting Class I differentials higher in each progressively more distant market to approximate the cost of transporting raw bulk milk from Eau Claire to each other. In addition, the difference in Class I price among markets in between will represent the cost of transporting milk between them.[21]

There is a second type of price alignment, blend price alignment, and the distinction is an important one. The Class I differential is the price set by the U.S. Department of Agriculture. These prices are aligned in the sense that they increase with distance from the milkshed. However, the price that really affects the flow of producer milk is the blend price, the price actually received by a farmer. This price is determined not only by the minimum prices set, but also by the utilization rate in the market. Blend prices will naturally align to reflect transportation costs between markets regardless of the actual level of Class I and Class II prices. This is because, although Class I differentials are set at fixed levels, the price mechanism operates to bring the system back into alignment when small supply-demand disequilibriums occur. If a "shortage" developed, Class I uses would have priority, thus forcing the utilization rate to increase. An increase in the utilization rate drives up the blend price. A higher blend price will attract increasingly distant suppliers into the market, which would then begin to drive the blend price back toward the level just high enough to compensate for transportation from one market to another. The term "shortage" is used very loosely here. Supply

---

[20] See, for example, Graf and Jacobson, *Resolving Grade B Conversion and Low Class I Utilization Pricing and Pooling Problems*, p. 7.

[21] For a map showing the Class I differentials in federal milk market orders as of January 1, 1976, see U.S. Department of Agriculture, Agricultural Marketing Service, *Summary of Major Provisions in Federal Milk Marketing Orders, January 1, 1976* (February 1976), p. 55.

would be short only in the sense that there was not enough surplus to drive the blend price back down to the level which would make it unprofitable to ship raw grade A milk from farms which normally sell in other market orders. It is quite conceivable that distant sources will sometimes be attracted even though the fluid needs of a market are more than adequately covered.

The Upper Midwest is the most efficient area of the country for milk production. For this reason, milk will ultimately come from this region if blend prices rise above the alignment. Therefore, this area must be the basing point. Blend prices increase in a pattern radiating from the Minnesota-Wisconsin area.[22]

Given that blend prices will align anyway, the question to be answered is at what level should the prices be set. This decision is implemented by setting the Class I differentials.

When the milk order program was first initiated, milk markets were correctly perceived as highly local in nature. The theory then was to have prices in the less efficient production areas set higher than they would be in the nation's milkshed in order to assure that an adequate supply of local milk for fluid needs would be produced. Now that the technology of transportation has improved to the point where milk can move in bulk as far as 2,000 miles, a limit was effectively placed on the level to which prices in less productive areas could be raised. The upper bound is the price in surplus regions plus the cost of moving that surplus to deficit areas. If Class I differentials were set so as to result in blend prices higher than this, milk could be economically delivered to the distant markets from the surplus production regions in the Upper Midwest. If prices went higher than this level, a market would become flooded with not only locally produced milk, but surplus milk from other regions as well. Thus, transportation alignment generates the greatest amount of local production without sacrificing the goal of insulating the local market from outside supplies.

Instead of simply setting local prices to reflect local conditions as could be done when milk markets were local by necessity, pricing policy must now take into account transportation alignment. Keeping markets insulated from outside milk in the face of improved transportability has necessitated raising the overall price level for milk. To establish strictly local self-sufficiency, prices must first be set in the least efficient region at a level high enough to bring forth adequate supply. Then, prices must be reduced consistent with transport costs as the base point, Eau Claire, Wisconsin, is approached.

---

[22] For a map showing average blend prices in federal order markets in 1975, see U.S. Department of Agriculture, FMOMS, *Annual Summary for 1975*, p. 68.

Florida is probably the least efficient milk production region in the country. The Class I differential in southern Florida is $3.15 per hundredweight. In an unregulated market, this difference would be well in excess of the cost of delivering grade A milk from Minnesota and Wisconsin. Such a price level would mean that Florida would be flooded not only with locally produced milk but with surplus milk delivered from faraway regions as well. One way to keep the distant milk out is to align Class I prices by transport costs back to the national milkshed. By doing this, producers in efficient regions are given prices that reflect, not their local conditions, but prices that are high enough to remove the incentive to ship to Florida. Producers all the way back to Wisconsin get a Florida price less transportation.

The problem with this plan, from the societal viewpoint, is apparent. It imposes prices characteristic of the most inefficient part of the country on the rest of the nation. Prices must be set in every order in conformity with the least productive area, so that consumers in the rest of the country pay prices reflective of the most inefficient area, subject only to reductions reflecting transport costs.

The ability of such a plan to raise the overall price of milk has been noted by dairy experts:

> Whenever price differences among markets are greater than the cost of moving milk, there is an incentive for milk to move. This incentive can be removed by aligning or adjusting prices so that their differences are identical to those in transportation costs. Once prices are aligned, the general price level among markets can be raised if all cooperatives raise prices at the same time.[23]

Most areas of the country are more efficient than the "Florida minus transport" price level that seems to prevail.[24] Prices set to give Florida local milk production yield a relatively modest surplus in that region. But Class I prices are diminished only by transport costs as one moves north. Nonetheless, the markets gain in efficiency at a rate that outstrips the transport adjustment. Thus, the higher than necessary Class I prices generate excess production for the reasons described above. Prices equivalent to Florida-less-freight in the Upper Midwest result in enormous surplus production there, approaching 200 percent in some cases. Noted authorities have indicated that a

---

[23] Ronald D. Knutson, *Cooperative Bargaining Developments in the Dairy Industry, 1960–1970*, U.S. Department of Agriculture, Farmer Cooperative Service, FCS Research Report No. 19 (August 1971), p. 17.

[24] See the map in U.S. Department of Agriculture, *FMOMS, Annual Summary for 1975*, pp. 44–45, which depicts surplus grade A production by regions.

surplus of 20 percent should be more than adequate in any federal order market.[25] This would be true even if each market was totally autonomous, that is, surplus milk was not or could not be brokered between markets. In 1975 the utilization rate across all federal order markets was 58 percent, meaning that there was a 72 percent surplus of grade A milk which had to be handled as surplus.

If the Class I differential in a federal order market located in the Upper Midwest were set at the level just necessary to cover the costs of converting a grade B farm to a grade A farm over the course of the marketing year, then grade A milk would be provided in that order market. A research report issued in June 1973 estimated that a 15-cents-per-hundredweight price difference was necessary in order to convert a grade B operation to a grade A. In 1973 the M-W manufacturing grade milk price was $6.30 per hundredweight.[26] The average blend price for the Minneapolis-St. Paul order in 1973 was $6.57 per hundredweight,[27] a difference of 27 cents. Thus, if the estimate of 15 cents is accurate, area milk producers will continue to convert to grade A production. However, the Class I differential in the Minneapolis-St. Paul order, as aligned from Florida, was a $1.06 per hundredweight.[28] Therefore, a considerable surplus of grade A milk was generated for that market order. Producers were willing to deliver milk to the Minneapolis-St. Paul market order until the utilization rate went low enough to force the blend price down toward the level where the costs of producing grade A milk were just covered by the difference between the M-W price and the blend price for that order.

The Class I differential in the Minneapolis-St. Paul order was still $1.06 as of January 1, 1976. The Class I differentials then increase with distance from Minneapolis-St. Paul. On January 1, 1976, the highest Class I differential was $3.15 in Southeastern Florida.[29] These higher Class I differentials then interact with local cost conditions to generate a surplus that in turn results in blend price align-

[25] Bartlett, "Bringing Federal Order Class I Pricing Up to Date and in Line with Antitrust Regulations," p. 7; Hugh L. Cook et al., Review of Eisenstadt, Philip, Robert T. Masson, and David Roddy, "An Economic Analysis of the Associated Milk Producers, Inc., Monopoly," Research Bulletin No. 2790 (Madison: University of Wisconsin, January 1976), p. 11.

[26] U.S. Department of Agriculture, FMOMS, Annual Summary for 1973 (June 1974), p. 77.

[27] Ibid., p. 68.

[28] U.S. Department of Agriculture, Summary of Major Provisions in Federal Milk Marketing Orders, January 1, 1973, p. 51.

[29] U.S. Department of Agriculture, Summary of Major Provisions in Federal Milk Marketing Orders, January 1, 1976, p. 55.

ment. The utilization rate in each market differs because of differences in the costs of production in the various federal order markets. Regions that have lower costs of production will have more milk produced at a given Class I differential, thus generating more excess supplies until the blend price is driven down to alignment. The most relatively efficient regions are generally those that have the highest amount of grade A surplus.

At least one observer has argued that the Class I differentials are entirely too high at present.[30] This argument is supported by the evidence of large surpluses in nearly all markets. Acknowledgments that chronic oversupply is a very serious problem of milk regulation permeate the literature on the subject.[31] This being the case, one must conclude that the size of Class I differentials has a severe impact on the price level of fluid milk. Excess supply indicates that the blend prices are too high. The blend prices could be lowered by decreasing the Class I differential. If alignment is maintained, however, milk prices can conceivably be raised to levels limited only by the consumer's willingness to pay. When the additional impact of Class I premiums that cooperatives charge is taken into account, the significance of the effect of Class I differentials on price levels is multiplied.

The Price Support Program. The federal price support program affects the price level of dairy products directly.[32] The Commodity Credit Corporation (CCC) supports the M-W manufacturing grade price at established levels by purchasing manufactured dairy products on the open market. This has an obvious impact on the price to manufacturing grade milk producers. The price support program also has a beneficial effect for fluid grade milk producers. As was explained above, the federal order system encourages a substantial overproduction of grade A milk. As was also explained, this overproduction must be channeled into manufacturing uses. The dairy products manufactured from grade A milk are identical to those made from grade B milk; these products are in direct competition with each other. As surplus grade A milk is channeled into manufacturing, the supply of manufactured dairy products increases, thus placing a downward pressure on the prices for such products. There will be a downward pressure on the M-W price, which is the base price for the federal order system. Each year, a support level, expressed as a per-

---

[30] Bartlett, "Bringing Federal Order Class I Pricing Up to Date and in Line with Antitrust Regulation."
[31] Ibid., p. 7.
[32] 7 U.S.C., section 1446(c).

centage of parity, is announced. The government is committed to purchase manufactured dairy products on the open market in order to keep the M-W price from falling below the support level. The government announces at what prices it will step in and purchase certain dairy products. Thus, the support program guarantees the grade A farmer, first, an ultimate outlet for his milk and, second, a minimum price level for the year. Because the Class II price is approximately equivalent to the M-W price by law, the price support program also supports the Class II price in federal milk orders.

In light of the large grade A surpluses that have existed in recent years, it is not surprising that CCC purchases have been substantial, reaching a thirteen-year high in fiscal 1975 with a net expenditure of $496.1 million. See Table 2-4 above. The table reveals that the government's intervention in the dairy market as a buyer has been very significant during the past fifteen years both in terms of dollars spent and percentage of production removed. In 1962 nearly 9 percent of total milk production was bought by the government, and removals of 5 percent to 7 percent are common. The impact of such large purchases on the prices consumers pay should be apparent.

4

EXISTENCE AND EXERCISE OF MARKET POWER BY DAIRY COOPERATIVES

The conduct by cooperatives has not been without a purpose and goal: the purpose, to obtain market power; the goal, to exercise it in order to reap monopoly rents. Market power is power over price, the ability to use discretion to charge a price over cost. Such power may result from government action, typically regulation, or from private firm activity. That some cooperatives have achieved significant market power can be clearly demonstrated: the existence of over-order Class I prices over time are proof of market power. These over-order prices cannot be explained as merely meeting costs incurred in providing services to buyers. The only explanation, both in theory and in practice, can be that the premiums extracted over the past ten years prove the existence and exercise of market power.

Existence of Over-Order Prices

The price set by the secretary of agriculture has been considered by him and others to be a minimum price: to the extent cooperatives have bargaining power, over-order prices can be extracted. Prior to 1956, prices in federal order markets essentially were the established price; market-wide premiums were rare. Over-order prices as a routine practice can be traced to the Detroit market in 1956.[1] From 1957

Editor's note: In the original report, Chapter 4 contains sections describing the goals of a dairy cooperative. Simply stated, the goals are: first to increase membership, and hence market share, in single federal order markets so that the local market "pool" (that is, the sum of all the money receipts from the sale of the order's milk supply) becomes the province of the members; second, to prevent entry of new milk into the local pool by isolating it from competing supplies.

[1] Milk Pricing Advisory Committee, *The Milk Pricing Problem*, Report to the U.S. Department of Agriculture, Part I (March 1972), p. 35.

through 1967, over-order prices in June were extracted in an average of 28 percent of the markets. For 1968–1971, that figure doubled to 60 percent.[2] As of January 1, 1975, there were over-order prices extracted in almost 90 percent of federal order markets.[3]

The organization of the standby pool on September 1, 1967, coincides with the successful implementation of persistent premiums of substantial size in many markets.[4] Over-order price levels reached significantly high levels in the fall of 1973, fell during the early months of 1974, and then climbed to substantial levels in the summer of 1974. This high level was substantially maintained throughout the end of 1974 and the beginning of 1975. See Figure 4-1. At the same time the simple average over-order charge was maintained at a high level (more than 75 cents), the Class I average price in all federal order markets increased significantly: from approximately $8.00 in 1973 to $9.35 in 1974.[5] It is curious that a study group attributed the sharp increase in over-order prices in 1974 as "due primarily to the decline in federal order Class I prices . . . and the efforts of the cooperative to maintain their selling prices."[6]

Starting in 1970, the practice was begun of charging a flat price to handlers. Previously, cooperatives had charged a flat premium over the order price, which meant that the selling price fluctuated as the order prices fluctuated.[7] The flat price approach assured the cooper-

---

[2] Robert T. Masson, "Some Issues of Cooperative Market Power, Cartelization, and the Capper-Volstead Act" (paper presented to the P.L.I. Conference on Cooperatives, December 1976), p. 8. Some premiums may have resulted from supply-demand adjustors.

[3] Report of the Interagency Task Force, *Price Impacts of Federal Market Order Programs*, U.S. Department of Agriculture, Farmer Cooperative Service, Special Report 12 (January 1975), pp. 11–12. Some of these over-order prices may be attributed to state-regulated prices that are higher than the federal order prices: in 1972, there were three states where this was true. See Milk Pricing Advisory Committee, *The Milk Pricing Problem*, Part I, p. 34.

[4] See Milk Pricing Advisory Committee, *The Milk Pricing Problem*, Part I, p. 38, which reports a decline in over-order prices somewhat after 1968, attributing the decline to sharply increasing Class I prices. Another explanation may be that AMPI, one of the largest cooperatives at the time, took its premiums off Class I milk, probably in response to publication of the fact that it was rebating to the Borden Company. Shortly thereafter, price controls were initiated, holding the price at a nonpremium level for some time. See Philip Eisenstadt, Robert T. Masson, and David Roddy, *An Economic Analysis of the Associated Milk Producers, Inc., Monopoly*, filed with the Court in United States v. Associated Milk Producers, Inc., 394 F. Supp. 29 (W.D. Mo. 1975), affirmed, 534 F.2d 113 (8th Cir. 1976), p. 183.

[5] See Table 3-2 above.

[6] Report of the Interagency Task Force, *Price Impacts of Federal Market Order Programs*, p. 12.

[7] Milk Pricing Advisory Committee, *The Milk Pricing Problem*, Part I, p. 37.

Figure 4-1

SIMPLE AVERAGE OVER-ORDER CHARGE BY THE DOMINANT COOPERATIVE IN THIRTY-ONE SELECTED CITIES

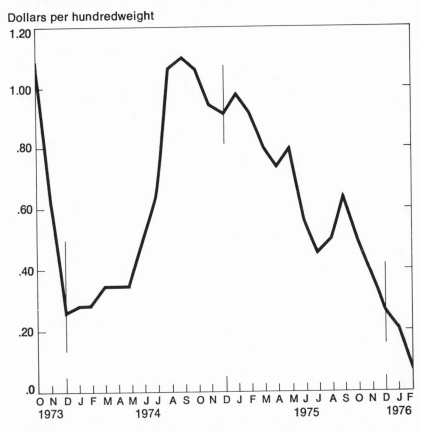

Dollars per hundredweight

Source: U.S. Department of Agriculture, Agricultural Marketing Service, Dairy Division.

Note: The thirty-one cities are:

Atlanta, Ga.	Houston, Texas	Pittsburgh, Pa.
Baltimore, Md.	Indianapolis, Ind.	Rock Island, Ill.
Boston, Mass.	Kansas City, Mo.	St. Louis, Mo.
Carbondale, Ill.	Louisville, Ky.	Salt Lake City, Utah
Chicago, Ill.	Miami, Fla.	Seattle, Wash.
Cleveland, Ohio	Milwaukee, Wis.	Spokane, Wash.
Dallas, Texas	Nashville, Tenn.	Springfield, Ill.
Denver, Colorado	Oklahoma City, Okla.	Washington, D.C.
Des Moines, Iowa	Omaha, Neb.	Waterloo, Iowa
Detroit, Michigan	Philadelphia, Pa.	
Hartford, Conn.	Phoenix, Ariz.	

atives of a fixed return and was not necessarily unwelcomed by handlers. Given that a premium would be extracted, this fixed pricing approach meant the handler was aware in advance of his supply costs for some period of time.[8] If a cooperative is able to extract a premium from one handler, normally it has the market power to do so market-wide. This meant that one handler knew other handlers—that is, his competitors—would be also paying the same price for their supplies. An "advance" toward more stability, from the handler's viewpoint, was initiated in the late 1970 to early 1971 practice of "bracketing." This practice automatically moved the negotiated price upward in 15-cent intervals when the M-W price rose by 15 cents.[9]

Premiums are reportedly less prevalent currently than they were even a year ago. In addition, litigation, both private and government, involving some dairy cooperatives has had an impact on some cooperative conduct. The efforts of the cooperative to obtain higher prices may now be directed to the less obvious attempts to raise order prices or support prices. However, the recent existence of substantial premiums for long periods of time, and the current experience of some premium extraction, must not be dismissed merely because levels are not as high as previously.

Premiums

Although superficially attractive, the argument that "superpool" premiums are merely compensation to the cooperatives for services rendered is a false one. The weakness of this claim is revealed by the pattern of premium experience, an understanding of the costs of the services rendered by the cooperative associations, and theoretical and practical market analysis.

Generally, there are three categories of services rendered by cooperatives: services for the producer, services for the handler, and market-wide services.[10] In a competitive world, it would be reason-

---

[8] High fixed prices, market-wide, are a mixed blessing for handlers. In fixing the price, cooperatives assure handlers that their competition is paying the same procurement price; thus, the handler does not have to be concerned with efficiencies in procurement. For example, AMPI stated in a brochure: "AMPI does not undercut price (*handlers buying from AMPI know that they are being treated fairly and are paying the same for milk as their competitors*), Associated Milk Producers Inc., AMPI '75: The Full Service Coop." This blessing is mixed because higher price levels means lower consumption, thus decreasing the volume a handler can sell.

[9] Milk Pricing Advisory Committee, *The Milk Pricing Problem*, Part I, p. 37.

[10] Hugh L. Cook et al., *Review of Eisenstadt, Philip, Robert T. Masson, and David Roddy, "An Economic Analysis of the AMPI Monopoly,"* Research Bulletin No. R2790 (Madison: University of Wisconsin, January 1976), p. 7.

able to expect the provider of services to the handler to negotiate with the handler in providing the services, including negotiating the price to the handler for the services. Such services are a value to the handler and are included in the marginal costs to the cooperative/producer in supplying the milk. In the category of handler services might be the delivery of milk to the handler's plant, quality control, split loads (delivery of less than a tankload), full-supply arrangements, and balancing market surplus.[11] However, it is unreasonable to expect to attribute to handlers the costs of all "services" provided by a cooperative, such as market-wide services.

The over-order payments that have been extracted by cooperatives from handlers have not been generally negotiated, nor have they been at levels which reasonably reflect the costs of the handlers' services. The customary practice of large cooperative associations or federations has been to announce a market-wide or area-wide price for milk in advance.[12] Generally, there is no negotiation on the level of over-order prices.[13] Although at some time, somewhere, a cooperative may have negotiated with some handler on the level of premium as reflecting the level of services provided, the practice is not widely reported in the literature, and can certainly be said to be the exception and not the rule.

In addition, many of the services rendered by cooperatives are services, or costs incurred, on milk delivered to the handler. An example would be the service of "daily balancing," that is, delivering to a handler on certain selected days. The cost to the cooperative for this type of service would arise out of all the milk so delivered, yet premiums are typically extracted on Class I sales.[14] However, the premiums charged do not reflect this: premiums are assessed on Class I milk regardless of the services provided. Robert T. Masson reasonably suggested the example of two handlers each on the same delivery schedule, one with a 65 percent Class I utilization, the other with 95 percent Class I utilization. The latter handler would pay the cooperative nearly 50 percent more in over-order "service" charges, even

---

[11] The last two services delineated are mentioned because they are now, or have been, frequently cited as important services provided by cooperatives. The need for these types of services is not endemic to milk marketing. Rather, the need arises because one dominant cooperative or federation desires to control market supplies and because a surplus is generated by the order system.

[12] See, for example, Central Milk Producers Cooperative, "Price Announcement," April 1976.

[13] An exception to this is the promise to protect a handler from lower prices paid by his competitors. See Cook et al., *Review of Eisenstadt, Philip, Robert T. Masson, and David Roddy*, p. 9.

[14] There are and have been Class II service charges but, when extracted, they have been generally at much lower levels than the Class I premium.

though he received the same special deliveries as the former handler.[15] This suspiciously suggests that the over-order charge is not for services rendered, but is merely a premium extracted.

Further, the level of premiums over the last ten-year period have not been in keeping with the cost of providing the services. A study done by R. E. Deiter, J. W. Gruebele, and E. M. Babb is one of the first efforts made to identify services provided by cooperatives, and their costs. In fact, their preliminary report states that "one of the major problems encountered in this part of the study is that the accounting records of many cooperatives is [sic] not adequate to identify the cost of individual services."[16] They report that it is easier to identify the costs of whole groups of services, although the method used to do so is not explained. Table 4-1 is excerpted from the Deiter-Gruebele-Babb report. The table shows the average cost of providing services by level of services and by size and type of cooperative in the North Central region in 1973. As the table demonstrates, the maximum average cost of providing *all* services is 15.10 cents per hundredweight for a cooperative handling more than 2 million hundredweight annually;[17] the average cost of all types and sizes of cooperatives of providing all three levels of services is 9.05 cents per hundredweight. However, the simple average premium extracted, over *all* markets and *all* types of cooperatives, for four selected months in 1973 was 26.75 cents as reported by USDA.[18] In one market, this same average was 57.25 cents per hundredweight.[19] Although the level of services, or the cost of providing these services may differ in other parts of the country, it seems quite unlikely that the national average cost of providing the national average level of services would be fully 292 percent of that same average of North Central cooperatives. Thus, the 1973 data reveals strong evidence that premiums charged did not merely reflect services rendered.

The premium data for 1974 is even more revealing. The all-market, simple average premium for four months was 72.25 cents per

---

[15] Masson, "Some Issues of Cooperative Market Power, Cartelization, and the Capper-Volstead Act," p. 10.

[16] R.E. Deiter, J.W. Gruebele, and E.M. Babb, "Services Provided by Dairy Cooperatives and What Do They Cost" (Preliminary paper presented at Mid-West Milk Marketing Conference, Columbus, Ohio, March 23–24, 1976), p. 7.

[17] Of course, the cost of providing all services cannot be reasonably charged to handlers.

[18] Attachment to letter from Robert W. March, deputy director, Dairy Division, Agricultural Marketing Service, U.S. Department of Agriculture, to Vicki Golden, attorney, Antitrust Division, U.S. Department of Justice, March 19, 1976.

[19] Ibid., p. 1, Market No. 13. (The market numbers were assigned randomly by USDA, and they do not correspond to federal market order numbers.)

Table 4-1

AVERAGE COST OF PROVIDING SERVICES BY LEVEL OF SERVICES FOR 31 DAIRY COOPERATIVES BY TYPE AND SIZE OF COOPERATIVE, IN THE NORTH CENTRAL REGION, 1973

(cents per hundredweight)

Cooperatives	Farm Level Cost	Market Level Cost	National Level Cost	Total Cost
All	4.60	4.25	0.20	9.50
Type				
Bargaining	3.35	2.80	0.10	6.25
Operating	4.04	3.10	0.34	7.48
Combination	4.61	5.22	0.20	10.03
Size				
More than 2,000,000	5.21	9.67	0.22	15.10
500,000–2,000,000	5.08	5.99	0.19	11.26
200,000–500,000	3.15	3.26	0.29	6.70
100,000–200,000	4.70	1.90	0.11	6.71
Less than 100,000	3.39	1.71	0.22	5.32

Source: R. E. Deiter, J. W. Gruebele, and E. M. Babb, "Services Provided by Dairy Cooperatives and What Do They Cost" (Preliminary paper presented at Mid-West Milk Marketing Conference, Columbus, Ohio, March 23–24, 1976), Table 10.

hundredweight. In one market this same average was $1.73 per hundredweight in over-order charges over the year.[20] The Deiter-Gruebele-Babb study did not cover 1974, but there is no evidence to suggest that cooperatives instituted wholesale increases in the level of services, nor were conditions drastically different in the dairy industry such that costs of providing services would rise to a level almost 275 percent of the previous alleged "cost" of providing services, 26.5 cents per hundredweight in 1973.

A point was recently made by Masson that raises another serious question about what over-order price charges really are:

> Furthermore, if one felt that premiums reflected valuable services, then one would expect the dollar spread between the retail price and the reported Class I price (including services charges) to be lower where there are coop premiums. This price spread would be lower by the cost sav-

---

[20] Ibid., p. 2, Market No. 23.

ings to the processor from taking services from the coop rather than providing the same services to himself.[21]

Masson cites "strong statistical evidence" that higher premiums are associated with higher farm-retail price spreads.[22]

It is not merely the average level of premiums, absence of negotiation, inequitable assessment, or higher farm-retail spread that indicate premiums are not merely, or substantially, service charges. For the years 1973–1975, the level of significance of positive association between concentration and premiums is one in ten thousand.[23] This correlation between the market share held by the dominant cooperative and the size of the premium extracted strongly indicates that over-order charges relate more to market power, which essentially amounts to control of Class I (graded) eligible milk in an order, than to the level of services provided.[24] Premiums have recently been much below the level previously extracted in some orders. See Figure 4-1. However, there is no evidence that the dominant cooperative in each order has ceased to provide the services, or lowered the level of services provided, in 1973–1974.

The Cause of Over-Order Prices

Numerous commentators on the dairy industry have attempted to explain the cause of the successful continued extraction of over-order prices by some cooperatives. Premiums on Class I sales alone indicated that they are not "functional" premiums, that is, reflective of a shortage or other market condition.[25] In fact, it is clear that premiums were extracted on Class I sales over the last ten to fifteen years

---

[21] Masson, "Some Issues of Cooperative Market Power, Cartelization, and the Capper-Volstead Act," p. 11.

[22] Ibid., citing C.N. Shaw, "Economic Effects of Resale Price Regulation on Market Performance in the Fluid Milk Industry" (Ph.D. diss., Pennsylvania State University, 1973), p. 59 (1969 data).

[23] "Statistical Analysis of Market Share and Over-Order Charges," on file at the U.S. Department of Justice, Antitrust Division, Economic Policy Office.

[24] The absence or significant lowering of premiums in markets where services are provided by cooperatives raises a serious question: Is milk being sold at less than the federal minimum order prices? This must be the conclusion if services are being provided at no or little over-order charge, where services previously were (supposedly) provided in exchange for a high level of premium. See Cook et al., *Review of Eisenstadt, Philip, Robert T. Masson, and David Roddy*, p. 7.

[25] Charles Bartlett, "Bringing Federal Order Class I Pricing Up to Date and in Line with Antitrust Regulations," *Illinois Agricultural Economics*, vol. 114 (January 1974), p. 6.

because of the comparatively inelastic demand for fluid milk at the retail level.[26]

As previously discussed, the federal order system plays a central role in aiding producers (or their cooperatives) in controlling the supply of milk for fluid use and the price charged for it. The Class II market price can fluctuate considerably, but the Class I differentials are fixed by law, and the existence of the fixed differential above the manufacturing-use milk price naturally pegs the volume of fluid-use milk that will be demanded. Supply of Class I milk is "controlled" indirectly by fixing the price that must be paid for it. This is the seeming paradox of the milk market monopoly but is really no paradox at all. In the "typical" monopoly situation, the seller has direct control over supply and increases price by restricting supply. There are no absolute supply controls on milk producers. The order system, however, by setting Class I prices artificially high, creates a noncompetitive return for farmers. Thus, the first source of monopoly prices for Class I milk is the Class I differentials created by the order system. These monopoly prices would exist with or without producer cooperatives.

Producer cooperatives have been able to increase monopoly rents by charging Class I premiums. An over-order premium may not be all monopoly profit,[27] but in this context the word "premium" will be used to denote that portion of an over-order charge that is pure monopoly in excess of the incremental costs of servicing the market. That portion includes the costs of monopolizing, nonincremental costs (such as advertising), and monopoly rents. The federal order system gives some assistance in maintaining and collecting these over-order premiums.

The most useful service provided to the cooperative by the order system per se is the auditing of handler uses of milk. Many early attempts by cooperatives to enforce classified pricing collapsed because handlers were not willing gratuitously to provide accurate information on their milk usage. Now, the government performs this policing function.

Other than the policing, the order system's assistance to coopera-

---

[26] Sheldon W. Williams et al., *Organization and Competition in the Midwest Dairy Industries* (Ames: Iowa State University Press, 1970), p. 75.

[27] Over-order charges can exist because there is a bona fide shortage of raw milk at the minimum order price. In this situation, no Class II milk would be sold in the area (except at the Class I price, including premium). Also, a service charge to the handler may be reflected only in the price of milk he buys. Only services that the handler would demand and receive at that price in an unregulated market can be deducted as a nonmonopolistic element of the over-order charge.

tives in achieving monopoly prices is more indirect. The key to monopoly prices is market share and market isolation. Because there are no absolute production controls, cooperatives must gain control of Class I eligible (graded) milk to their markets. To the extent the order system furthers the goals of the cooperative in these areas, it is important for premium extraction.

The extraction of over-order prices on Class I sales, referred to as a "bargaining success" by one commentator, is clearly the result of the efforts of cooperatives: "joint activity through federated bargaining groups," market share growth through mergers, "control of supply," and "other methods."[28] Observations of where premiums have been extracted support the conclusion that the merger/federation activity of cooperatives, and their attempts to control Class I eligible supply to a market have led to over-order pricing. For example, the Milk Pricing Advisory Committee noted in 1972 that the lower level of premiums in the North Central area was attributed to a *larger number* of cooperatives competing. It was noted in that report that the North Central area, in comparison with areas like the South where over-order prices were substantial, had a large number of cooperatives competing, a small fluid market, and a large grade A surplus available. It further noted that the relatively low over-order prices obtained in some parts of the Northeast and West were attributable to insufficient consolidation of cooperative activity.[29]

There can be little doubt about the source of monopoly power: control of supply movement of graded milk through the order system, achieved through merger activity, federations, the standby pool, full-supply contracts, and other tactics. If premium-extracting cooperatives had not been able to keep lower-priced grade A milk out of their markets (that is, make such milk not economically accessible to their handlers), premiums could not have been sustained at such high levels over so long a period of time.

Because of the importance of this conclusion, we will analyze the issue from the negative to determine if the conclusion is correct. Assuming that milk markets are competitive, we raise the question: Can the over-order prices that have been experienced be rationalized with a competitive market?[30]

---

[28] Williams et al., *Organization and Competition in the Midwest Dairy Industries,* p. 75. See also Report of the Interagency Task Force, *Price Impacts of Federal Market Order Programs,* p. 6.

[29] Milk Pricing Advisory Committee, *The Milk Pricing Problem,* Part I, pp. 37–39.

[30] For purposes of this analysis, a competitive market is one in which a cooperative lacks dominant market power. The source of this analysis is in Masson, "Some Issues of Cooperative Market Power, Cartelization, and the Capper-Volstead Act," n. 65.

In the federal order markets, a producer receives the same (blend) price for his grade A milk regardless of whether it is used as Class I or Class II by the handler. If farmers supplying Class I handlers were receiving a premium, and similarly situated farmers supplying Class II handlers were not receiving a premium,[31] the market processes of a competitive market would erode the Class I premiums or raise a Class II premium, until returns to farmers were equal between the two markets. Farmers supplying the lower-return Class II market will always find it advantageous to offer their milk at a price about that for Class II, but less than the over-order Class I price. The Class I market is economically more attractive, and, because the market is limited (that is, only a certain quantity will be taken at a given price), the former Class II farmer will undercut the going Class I price to gain a share of the market that yields a higher return. This process—competition—would continue until Class I and Class II markets for milk returned the same amount to farmers. If a shortage existed in the competitive market, one would expect to see Class II handlers offering a premium to obtain supplies. If supplies were so short that all demand could not be met, the price paid, for both Class I and Class II milk, would rise until the supply available satisfied the demand desired at the higher price.

These results must occur in a competitive market because there is no product differentiation between Class I and Class II milk when sold to the processor. The only reason there are two or more class prices now is because there is regulation. And the only reason there is a premium, over substantial periods of time, on Class I sales in excess of those on Class II sales is because the regulated markets are not "competitive": the producers, through their cooperatives, must have market power to be able to extract premiums on Class I milk.

Cooperatives frequently respond to this type of analysis by arguing that they have assumed the responsibility of supply balancing within a market area by operating Class II processing plants. Cooperatives claim that these plants are frequently operated at a loss.[32] Cooperatives argue that because they lose money on their Class II operations (which, they argue, are a benefit to the market), they should be compensated for their costs in providing this service by receiving Class I premiums. Many cooperatives have been successful in extracting such payments. In a competitive market, how-

---

[31] The same analysis would apply if both received premiums, but at different levels.

[32] Such operations may merely be operating at lower but positive net revenues from Class II operations than from Class I sales. The analyses would remain the same in a competitive market, prices (or net revenues) will equilibrate.

ever, a cooperative could not extract a Class I premium over a long period of time if any of their milk supply was being processed at a loss to them. When there are Class I premiums, a cooperative which is processing Class II milk at a loss can offer such milk to a Class I processor, at even no premium, and be in a better economic situation than before. Any cooperative which states that it processes Class II milk at a loss and charges a premium on Class I milk, over a substantial period of time, is stating that it has market power.

That cooperatives claim they should be reimbursed is an interesting twist of economic analysis. In a competitive market, the cooperative that is *least* efficient in marketing its milk to Class I handlers would have the most surplus to dispose of. "The cost of disposing of the surplus milk would be the burden imposed by the market place on the least efficient competitor."[33] And yet, in the fluid milk markets, cooperatives have urged that they should be compensated for providing a "service" to the market by handling the very same surplus.

If markets were competitive, the surplus-handling cooperatives would always offer to sell their surplus to Class I handlers for less than the going over-order price, and these cooperatives would earn more money than they would by processing the surplus into Class II products at a loss. Masson notes:

> A common defense for not doing so is that if they did, competitors would meet the price, prices would fall and (net) revenues would decrease. But this is a statement that "We cannot lower price ourselves without moving down an inelastic demand curve." This is the classic definition of market power.[34]

Thus, cooperatives with market power tolerate Class II operational losses in order to reap some Class I premiums.

The relationship between the Class II surplus processed by the cooperatives and the Class I premiums extracted by the cooperatives is key to understanding the market power of the cooperatives.

> To monopolize the milk markets and get a Class I premium requires *control over the milk that can most logically serve the market*. The key to getting the power necessary to charge a Class I premium is control over the milk which can undercut a premium price when one is imposed. Since Class II milk sales will seldom obtain a premium, *substantial*

---

[33] Masson, "Some Issues of Cooperative Market Power, Cartelization, and the Capper-Volstead Act," p. 6.
[34] Ibid.

uncontrolled milk going into Class II use is a threat to the ability to charge premiums. Dairy economists and coops cite supply control as crucial to "bargaining power" (only a "good" in their eyes). Supply control means controlling enough of the grade "A" milk, both Class I *and Class II* so as to assure that a processor facing a Class I premium cannot simply turn to a coop losing money on Class II operations and get a more than willing alternative supply with a lower premium. "Bargaining power" is equivalent to "market power". Thus, control of the market surplus is crucial to monopoly control. *Surplus balancing becomes not a cost accruing to the least effective competitor, but rather a cost of gaining market control and market power!* If we were to reimburse coops for Class II processing losses in this case we would be paying for, rewarding, and encouraging monopoly power.[35]

Thus, the operation of Class II processing plants at a loss by cooperatives is no service to the market; rather, it is a crucial element in achieving and maintaining market power.

Implications of Over-Order Prices

The extraction of over-order prices raises serious questions about the role of the federal order system. Even if order prices are conceded to be merely minimum prices, the legislative history quite clearly sets forth Congress' intent that orders not continue—certainly not year after year—with prices in excess of that level determined by the secretary to achieve the purposes of the Agricultural Adjustment Act.[36] Orders have continued, however, despite the existence of substantial premiums extracted by cooperatives in many markets:

> In these markets, the role of the Federal order pricing has tended to shift from price establishment to undergirding cooperative bargaining efforts and Federal order minimum prices are no longer the actual prices handlers pay for milk.[37]

This "success" of cooperatives raises serious questions about the role of federal orders; however, such questions are apparently not so serious from USDA's point of view. Since 1958, USDA has not seriously considered withdrawing an order because of over-order prices. The department considered suspending the Philadelphia order in 1958 because the state-regulated prices were greater than Class I prices.

---

[35] Ibid., p. 7 (emphasis added, except for third emphasis).

[36] See Chapter 1 above; 7 U.S.C. 608c(18).

[37] Milk Pricing Advisory Committee, *The Milk Pricing Problem*, Part I, p. 2.

Apparently, from the department's attitude, negotiation for premiums has been accepted as a "legitimate bargaining" activity.[38]

The highly regarded Nourse Committee, however, in its study of the dairy industry at a time when pervasive and persistent over-order pricing was really in its early stages (1962), strongly suggested that orders ought to be suspended in the face of persistent premiums:

> It may be argued under a mechanistic theory of market behavior, that, if free collective bargaining results in over-pricing, the process will be self-correcting. But, experience shows that, with the less than completely free market conditions provided by the Secretary's order and with dairy price supports, monopoloid distortions of the market and intermarket price structure may persist indefinitely. This would defeat the basic purpose of the order system to achieve as fully and promptly as possible a national milk price structure that would be internally consistent, serve consumers' needs, and promote optimum allocation of the nation's productive resources. *We, therefore, recommend that, in markets where negotiated marketwide premiums (or higher-than-order prices imposed by state agencies) exist, the Department institute hearings to review the level of Class I prices and any limitations on free access to the market.* If, thereafter, such premiums still persist consideration should be given to suspension of the pricing and pooling provisions of the order.[39]

Nothing about the Nourse Committee observations on the order system has changed. In fact, their observation has proved to be quite correct. Yet, there have never been any hearings to consider the source of over-order prices, despite four petitions to the secretary,

---

[38] Ibid., pp. 39–40. There was recently pending a petition to the secretary under section 2 of the Capper-Volstead Act, alleging that the extraction of substantial over-order prices for a period of time amounts to undue price enhancement. The relief sought was termination of the orders in question. See National Consumers Congress, *Petition for Initiation of Proceedings Under Section 2 of the Capper-Volstead Act, Before the Secretary of Agriculture*, U.S. Department of Agriculture (February 2, 1976). The USDA's response was that "further inquiry into the question of undue price enhancement should be made," and the department issued a questionnaire to nine cooperatives concerning their pricing policies. See Letter to John Cary Sims, Esq., from James D. Keast, chairman, Capper-Volstead Committee, U.S. Department of Agriculture, April 5, 1976. In December it was reported that the Department of Agriculture had rejected the petition. *Washington Post*, December 31, 1976.

[39] Federal Milk Order Study Committee, *Report to the Secretary of Agriculture*, U.S. Department of Agriculture (December 1962), p. 99 (emphasis added).

and the secretary has never issued a complaint under section 2 of the Capper-Volstead Act.[40]

Conclusion

Industry observers openly attribute extraction of premiums on Class I sales to successful cooperative "bargaining power." As Congress predicted, dairy cooperatives have been unable to control the production output by each individual farmer. However, to the extent that they have been able to control the *movement* of the grade A supply of milk in an order, they are able to eliminate competition and, by using the order prices as a floor, have been able to extract over-order payments. The ability to control the movement of milk has been achieved in great measure through mergers, federations (of which ARSPC is a unique type), and other collective activities. Because of the relatively free rein cooperatives had in merger activity in the 1960s, they have been able to achieve monopolistic market power in various regional markets. Merger is a substantial advantage to a corporation or cooperative in achieving market power, because it increases production or market share at the same time that it eliminates competition. Federations, of course, are a less permanent form of achieving market power, but they have served their purpose for cooperatives, particularly in controlling the movement of northern surplus milk.

Thus, although Congress felt confident in creating an antitrust exemption for cooperative and federation activity, in part because absence of production control would act as a check against exposing the public to an agricultural monopoly, the evils of just such a situation have been achieved in many markets, largely through merger and federation activity. In addition, the federal order system, whose provisions have on occasion been used in a predatory way, has also been instrumental in preserving the market power of dairy cooperatives. Other anticompetitive behavior has also been observed. Without overstatement, it is clear that the limited potential for anticompetitive results foreseen by Congress when enacting the Capper-Volstead Act more than fifty years ago has in fact been exceeded by cooperative conduct in the United States in the 1960s and 1970s. The inherent checks on agricultural monopoly—unrestrained production and splintering from cooperatives—have not been effective in milk.

The "bargaining power" of cooperatives is actually market

---

[40] National Consumers Congress, *Petition for Initiation of Proceedings under Section 2 of the Capper-Volstead Act*, pp. 11–12.

power: the power to raise price. The existence of persistent and substantial over-order prices by cooperatives with significant market share is proof of their market power. Characterization of premiums as service charges is a ruse. The charges have been consistently in excess of the cost of services provided, and the principal "service" provided, balancing surplus, is not a service; rather, it is a means of controlling Class I eligible milk to the market, a key to market power. Some cooperatives, making generous use of their Capper-Volstead exemption and the federal order system, have achieved and exercised monopoly power. Without the federal system, none of this would likely have occurred and certainly would not have been allowed to persist.

5

COSTS OF MILK REGULATION

Recent literature has attempted to place a dollar value on the costs of maintaining regulation of milk marketing. All such studies use an unregulated system as the standard against which the current marketing system is evaluated. It should be noted that these studies purport to measure only the cost associated with milk regulation; they do not claim to net out the cost against any social benefit of milk regulation.[1] However, it is against the costs discussed in this part that any benefits of the system that are derived must be balanced in understanding the net effect. This discussion will serve only as a general explanation of the results and methodology employed by various researchers. A complete and comprehensive understanding of the costs of milk regulation can only be had by referring to the original studies.

The studies deal with two types of social impacts: deadweight social loss and transfer payments. A deadweight social loss is the net value of goods and services wasted or not produced because of deviations from ideal competitive market performance. It represents an unequivocal loss of assets to society. Transfer payments, on the other hand, refer simply to redistribution of wealth. Money is transferred from one identifiable economic group to another as a result of deviations from a competitive market norm. Understandably, deadweight losses can be viewed as the more serious problem. Transfer payments are more properly characterized as a political issue involving the relative welfare of subgroups within the society. However, the efficiency with which a given transfer is accomplished is an issue which can give rise to social costs.

Various features of milk regulation have been evaluated independently by the studies, and each will be separately reviewed. The

---

[1] Benefits of the regulation are analyzed, although not in quantitative dollar value terms, in chapter 6.

first section will look at the cost of the federal order system, given the state of technology and other factors as constant. The next section will deal with costs associated with the monopolization of raw milk supply by cooperatives. Finally, other aspects of milk regulation will be examined, especially the price support program.

An overview of the studies under review indicates that the total deadweight social loss attributable solely to the federal order system is, by the most conservative estimate, $50 million a year. The federal order system also results in transfer payments of between $180 million and $230 million from fluid milk consumers, of which $110 million to $140 million goes to subsidizing Class II consumers and the remaining $50 million to $100 million goes to producers of raw milk. Deadweight loss because of monopolization, exclusive of order system costs, is in the vicinity of $55 million a year, with transfer payments from milk consumers to milk producers in the range of $150 million to $200 million. Elimination of state regulation and prohibitions on reconstituted milk could save roughly $150 million in welfare loss; and $250 million in transfer payments. The costs of the price support system are dependent on the percentage of parity at which the support price is set. Estimates of welfare loss range from $0 at 75 percent of parity to $94 million at 90 percent of parity. Transfer payments with a support price of 90 percent of parity are calculated at $850 million. These estimates are the results of several different studies employing different assumptions and different methodologies. Therefore, it would be inappropriate to draw any conclusion based upon the sum total of their estimates.

Social Costs of the Federal Order System

There are both deadweight losses and transfer payments that are attributable to the federal order system. They will be treated in turn.

Deadweight Losses. Deadweight loss resulting from the federal order system has been estimated by Richard Ippolito and Robert Masson.[2] Their research paper centered on the social costs of the federal order system alone. In order to obtain their estimate, they made several simplifying assumptions. The most important of these included the aggregation of all federal order markets into one model federal order market. This was done because Class II prices are fairly constant throughout the country, and Class I differentials would be fairly con-

---

[2] Richard Ippolito and Robert T. Masson, "The Social Costs of Federal Regulation of Milk" (unpublished paper, January 1976).

Figure 5-1

EQUILIBRIUM IN AGGREGATED FEDERAL MILK ORDERS

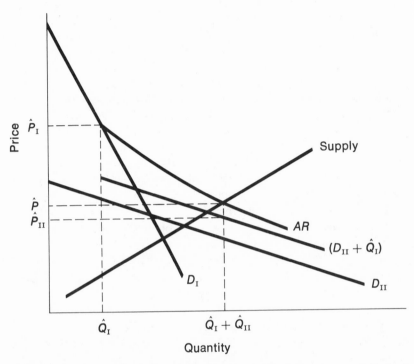

Source: Richard Ippolito and Robert Masson, "The Social Costs of Federal Regulation of Milk" (unpublished paper, January 1976), Figure 2.

stant throughout the country once they were netted of transportation costs from the Upper Midwest. In addition, their model aggregates milk demand and supply on an annual basis, even though supply varies considerably within the year. Finally, grade A and grade B milk were aggregated in the model, treating them as homogeneous products after allowing a cost difference for the grade B milk. The authors believe that the sum of these simplifications biases their results in a downward direction.[3]

Figure 5-1 is a graphic representation of the aggregated federal order model used by Ippolito and Masson. The demand for Class I milk is represented as fairly inelastic, with a much more elastic de-

---

[3] Ibid., appendix.

mand for Class II milk. The model assumes that Class I demand is fulfilled first; milk production in excess of this demand ("surplus") is directed into Class II uses. Figure 5-2 further breaks down the various types of social loss they measured.

The first type of deadweight loss to be examined under the federal order system is that resulting from the misallocation of milk between its alternative uses. In particular, consumers are willing to pay more for milk processed for fluid use than the cost of producing it. In federal order markets the price of milk for fluid use is kept well above the cost of producing it, and therefore well above the price that would prevail in an unregulated system. The increased price can be shown to result in a lower consumption. This social loss is represented graphically by the shaded area in Figure 5-2(A). The counterpart to the reduced consumption of milk for fluid use is the "excessive" milk directed to Class II uses compared to what would be consumed at the price that would prevail in an unregulated system. The social loss from this source is represented by the shaded area in Figure 5-2(B). Ippolito and Masson have estimated the social loss attributable to misallocation of consumption to be as high as $13.1 million a year in the short run, $6.1 million a year in the long run. The complete range of their estimates can be found in Table 5-1 under different assumptions about the nature of the market for milk, namely, various combinations of supply and demand elasticities.

In addition to the deadweight loss resulting from misallocation of resources generated by the classified pricing system, there is a deadweight loss associated with overproduction of grade A milk caused by the blend price feature of milk marketing regulations. Maximum estimates of this loss approach $30 million annually in the long run. The blend price mechanism creates an overproduction of grade A milk in the sense that producers receive more for their grade A raw milk than manufacturing handlers pay for it. The blend price, the price received by producers, exceeds the price that would prevail in an unregulated market. That unregulated price is taken as a measure of the true value of milk at the output that would be produced at that unregulated price. A deadweight loss arises because the resources used in producing milk in excess of the competitive level of output (Q°) exceed the value that consumers place on this additional output. The dollar loss is measured as the difference between the blend price and the competitive price for all milk produced above the competitive level of output. See the dark shaded areas in Figure 5-2(C). Again, a summary of Ippolito and Masson's findings on the amount of overproduction deadweight loss for a range of supply and

Figure 5-2
THE SOCIAL COST OF MILK REGULATION

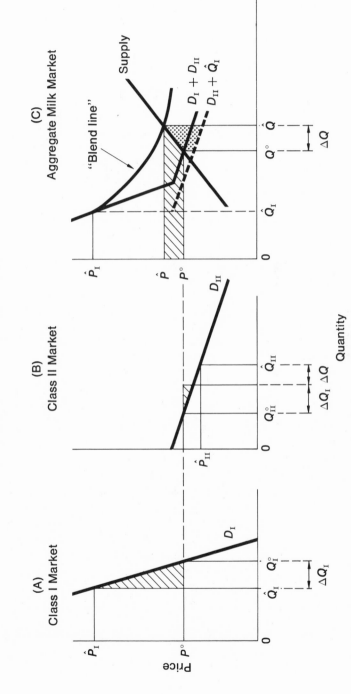

Source: Ippolito and Masson, "The Social Costs of Federal Regulation of Milk," Figure 3.

101

Table 5-1

ESTIMATES OF THE SOCIAL COST OF MILK REGULATION

($\gamma = 0.25$; estimates in millions of dollars)

Class II Demand Elasticity	Class I Demand Elasticity					
	Short-run supply elasticity $\varepsilon = 0.5$			Long-run supply elasticity $\varepsilon = 5.0$		
	−0.10	−0.32	−0.70	−0.10	−0.32	−0.70
−0.46	25.8 (0.04; 0.10)	15.4 (0.21; 0.10)		7.2 (0.08; 0.47)	6.7 (0.38; 0.36)	
−1.00	46.6 (0.03; 0.09)	37.8 (0.10; 0.10)	26.2 (0.30; 0.09)	15.3 (0.04; 0.48)	15.0 (0.14; 0.46)	14.4 (0.40; 0.36)
−2.00	66.9 (0.02; 0.09)	61.1 (0.08; 0.09)	52.8 (0.19; 0.09)	28.5 (0.02; 0.49)	28.6 (0.08; 0.48)	28.6 (0.18; 0.45)
−5.00	88.9 (0.02; 0.09)	88.7 (0.03; 0.09)	87.1 (0.15; 0.09)	58.4 (0.02; 0.50)	59.5 (0.05; 0.49)	61.2 (0.10; 0.48)

Note: Numbers in parentheses are the proportions of social cost attributable to misallocation of consumption and to overexpansion of output.

Source: Richard Ippolito and Robert T. Masson, "The Social Costs of Federal Regulation of Milk" (unpublished paper, January 1976), Table 1.

demand elasticities representing long-run and short-run estimates is contained in Table 5-1.

The final deadweight social loss attributed to the federal order system is that of rent erosion. The existence of this cost is based on several articles cited by Ippolito and Masson.[4] The federal regulation creates monopoly rents or returns for producers. See the light shaded area in Figure 5-2(C). However, these rents are partially abrogated by expenses incurred in maintaining the regulation. In other words, the transfer payments created by the federal regulation are not deadweight losses, but the expenses incurred in instituting and maintaining the federal regulation are. Rent erosion is the cost of gaining transfer payments. If, for example, monopoly pricing increases the prices paid by consumers a total of $300, of which $200 is transferred to suppliers and $100 is expended in maintaining the monopoly prices, there is $100 of rent erosion, which is a deadweight loss, and $200 of transfer payments. The Ippolito-Masson estimates of deadweight loss because of rent erosion range as high as $79 million in the long run, based on an estimate of 25 percent erosion of total monopoly rents generated by milk regulation.

Included in the category of rent erosion is the expense of operating the federal order market system. The market order system is financed by an assessment on each hundredweight of milk sold. The assessments vary from order to order, ranging from 1.5 cents to 5 cents per hundredweight. Assessments of 3 cents and 4 cents are quite common. The 1976 budget for the operation of the federal order system places the annual cost at $22.7 million.[5] This, of course, must be categorized as a deadweight loss suffered, as contrasted with an unregulated system in which such an expense would not be incurred. Ippolito and Masson used this expense as a rough cross-check on their estimate of 25 percent rent erosion. They calculated the expense of the federal order system to be $26 million in 1973. By comparing this administration expense with their long-run rent estimates, they found the rent erosion proportion to be 0.23, very close to their 25 percent assumption. Deadweight loss because of rent erosion is compiled along with the other deadweight losses in Table 5-1.[6] It should be noted that, in general, rent erosion represents the

---

[4] Ibid., p. 10.

[5] Attachment to a letter from Robert W. March, deputy director, Dairy Division, Agricultural Marketing Services, U.S. Department of Agriculture, to Vicki Golden, attorney, U.S. Department of Justice, March 19, 1976.

[6] Because these deadweight losses are reduced in situations where Class II demand is assumed to be more inelastic but the expense of operating the federal order system is constant, Ippolito and Masson claim that their deadweight loss

single most significant deadweight loss attributable to federal milk regulation. In many cases, rent erosion accounts for more than half of the deadweight losses.

As can be inferred from Table 5-1, there is a range of possibilities for the true deadweight social loss that Ippolito and Masson sought to estimate. However, the authors, in their judgment, assert that a conservative estimate of the long-run annual loss because of milk regulation is $50 million.

John E. Kwoka has also conducted a study of the costs of the federal milk marketing order system as compared to an unregulated market using data from 1960 and 1970.[7] Unlike Ippolito and Masson, Kwoka estimated social costs in individual order markets and then aggregated his findings. Ippolito and Masson had used an aggregate model in the first instance. In addition, Kwoka made no attempt to estimate rent erosion as part of the social cost of the order system. He does, however, estimate misallocation and overproduction costs. Expressly assuming that, in an unregulated market, there would be a uniform price for grade A milk equal to the current Class II price, and impliedly assuming that import quotas would not be effective constraints, Kwoka estimates the total deadweight loss at $202 million annually. This is considerably higher than the Ippolito-Masson estimate for the same market distortions. The difference may arise out of the fact that Kwoka's estimate is a short-run estimate. In addition, it is considered unlikely that a uniform price for grade A milk in an unregulated market would fall all the way to the current Class II level, as Kwoka has assumed.

Transfer Payments. Transfer payments are not to be confused with deadweight losses: money is not lost; rather, it is transferred from one economic group to another. A calculation of transfer payments begins by multiplying actual production by the competitive price for grade A raw milk that would be expected to prevail in an unregulated system. This price must be estimated from a model. Total actual production multiplied by the estimated price yields a total revenue figure. This is then compared with actual Class I volume multiplied by the actual Class I price; the difference is the Class I transfer. The same comparison is made for Class II volume to obtain the Class II transfer. The net of these two transfers is the monopoly rent to producers. The net rent to producers is the overcharge to Class I consumers less subsidies to Class II consumers. If it is accepted that Class I fluid milk is

estimates may be biased downward. Ippolito and Masson, "The Social Costs of Federal Regulation of Milk," p. 15.
[7] John E. Kwoka, "Pricing under Federal Milk Market Regulation: Theory, Objectives, and Impact" (unpublished paper, 1975).

Table 5-2
TRANSFERS ASSOCIATED WITH REGULATION
OF MILK BY PRICE DISCRIMINATION
($\varepsilon = 5.0$; estimates in millions of dollars)

η_I	η_{II}	Tax on Class I Milk	Subsidy to Class II Milk	Rent to Producers[a]
−0.10	−2.00	192.0	134.0	56.0
	−5.00	229.5	107.8	113.2
−0.32	−2.00	189.0	136.7	50.7
	−5.00	229.0	108.3	112.4
−0.70	−2.00	184.0	141.0	42.0
	−5.00	223.0	114.1	102.3

[a] Rent to producers is equal to the tax on Class I consumers net of the subsidy to Class II consumers and net of a portion of the incremental costs of expanding total milk output.
Source: Ippolito and Masson, "The Social Costs of Federal Regulation of Milk," Table 2.

properly characterized as a necessity, and manufactured products such as cheese are considered luxury items, then the regressive impact of milk regulation on consumers becomes apparent. The findings of Ippolito and Masson are summarized in Table 5-2 for various estimates of demand elasticity for Class I and Class II milk. The supply elasticity is taken as 5.0, indicating a long-run assumption. Class I consumer overcharges range between $108 million a year and $141 million a year. Net monopoly transfer to producers would be obtained by subtracting the subsidies from the overcharges. This yields a net transfer from consumers to producers in the range of $100 million annually.

Dairy farmers are not a monolithic group within which benefits from transfers are shared equitably. Some benefit considerably, others are actually harmed by the order system. Since their January 1976 draft, Ippolito and Masson have done additional work on the social costs of milk regulation.[8] This later research alters the model somewhat, in that federal *and state* regulation are aggregated. This model loses some ability to differentiate between the effects of state and federal regulation, but it has the added capacity to look more closely at other relationships, especially the relative impact of regulation on grade A and grade B producers. Some estimates in the latter paper

[8] Richard Ippolito and Robert T. Masson, "The Social Costs of Federal Regulation of Milk" (unpublished paper, October 1976).

are slightly more conservative because of more conservative supply elasticity estimates.

The net transfer from consumers to producers was still found to be about $100 million a year, but this was further segmented between the impact on regulated grade A producers and the impact on unregulated grade B producers. Gross transfers to grade A producers was found to be $211 million a year, while transfers *from* grade B producers was $105.2 million.[9] This still nets out to a total net transfer from consumers to producers of about $100 million, but grade A producers benefit greatly from the transfer while grade B producers actually lose. The disadvantaged producers are located primarily in Minnesota and Wisconsin. Grade B operations are almost uniformly smaller farms, which raises a serious equity question on the incidence of the impact of regulation.

Kwoka also estimated the magnitude of transfer payments occasioned by the federal order system by measuring overcharges to Class I consumers. His estimate, based on 1970 data, is $805 million a year. Again, Kwoka was operating under the assumptions detailed above, which explain in part the significantly higher estimate he makes.

Social Costs of Monopoly Pricing by Dairy Cooperatives

In addition to the social costs of the federal order system itself, Ippolito and Masson explore the costs associated with monopolistic control of milk supply by dairy cooperatives. Ippolito and Masson maintain that the federal order system is a crucial cause of the ability of dairy cooperatives to monopolize.[10] However, they have estimated the magnitude of the social loss because of this problem exclusive of any costs arising out of the order system. Monopoly distortion was measured by taking the amounts of over-order Class I charges and working them into their model simply as increments to the Class I differentials. This treatment would, of course, amplify the misallocation and over-production distortions previously discussed. The increased Class I prices further restrict the quantity milk handlers are willing to buy and, to the extent that the additional Class I charges are reflected in a higher blend price paid by the cooperative to its members (called a "reblend" price), member producers will be encouraged to further increase their production because of the still higher price they will receive. Ippolito and Masson estimate this increased deadweight loss

---

[9] Ibid., p. 51.

[10] Ippolito and Masson, "The Social Costs of Federal Regulation of Milk," n. 17. See also Robert T. Masson and Philip Eisenstadt, "Regulation as a source of Monopoly: A Case Study in Milk" (paper presented to the Atlantic Economic Society Annual Meetings, 1975).

from monopoly at $60 million ($15 million misallocation and over-production loss; $45 million rent erosion).[11]

Additional transfer payments resulting from monopoly control are estimated by Ippolito and Masson at $150 million to $200 million a year.[12] Presumably, this was calculated as the sum of over-order charges.

Costs of the Price Support Program

There are conceptually similar deadweight loss and transfer payments which arise out of the operation of the federal price support program. The standard of comparison is a market system with no price support program. Again, only the costs are quantified; any benefits attributed to a price support program must be netted against those cost estimates in assessing the wisdom of the program. The studies under review here deal only with the magnitude of the costs.

The price support program and the federal order market system are distinct and separate programs. Despite the fact that they are administered separately, they function in a highly interrelated manner. The price support program supports the price of grade B manufacturing milk, the federal order system sets market order grade A prices. The grade B price of milk is, however, the primary base price used in calculating federal order prices: thus the interrelationship.

Although the Agricultural Adjustment Act authorizes federal marketing orders for many commodities, only milk orders are authorized to set prices. Section 2 of the Agricultural Adjustment Act states that one of the goals of federal market orders is to maintain parity prices to producers.[13] This broad imperative is modified in the case of milk: section 8(c)(18) states that the secretary of agriculture, in setting federal milk order prices, shall first ascertain the parity price level for milk. Then, if the secretary determines that "the parity prices of such commodities are not reasonable in view of the price of feeds, the available supply of feeds, and other economic conditions which affect market supply and demand for milk and its products in the marketing area to which the contemplated agreement, order, or amendment relates, he shall fix such prices as he finds will reflect such factors, insure a sufficient quantity of pure and wholesome milk, and be in the public interest." At present, milk order prices are at a level lower than parity, as defined in 7 U.S.C., section 1301(a)(1)A.

---

[11] Ippolito and Masson, "The Social Costs of Federal Regulation of Milk," n. 17. Rent erosion was calculated at 25 percent of total monopoly rents generated.

[12] Ibid., n. 18.

[13] 7 U.S.C., section 602.

Support prices are likewise below the parity level. Section 1446(c) requires that the support price for milk be set, at the secretary of agriculture's discretion, between 75 percent and 90 percent of the parity price definition. With respect to milk, the parity price definition is considered too high for a number of reasons, including the dramatic increases in dairy farm productivity since the 1920s. The social costs of the price support program depend upon at what percentage of parity the current support price is pegged. The higher the support level, the higher the social costs.

Deadweight Loss. Boyd M. Buxton and Jerome W. Hammond have made estimates of the deadweight loss generated by the price support system.[14] Their analysis assumes the existence of the federal order system. They measure social costs by using the federal order equilibrium price which would exist if there were no price support system. This is higher than the price that would prevail in a totally unregulated market. As noted above, the federal order system encourages an overproduction of grade A milk that must be diverted into Class II use. The increased supply of Class II milk creates a downward pressure on all milk used for manufacturing purposes, including grade B milk. There is a limit on how far the grade B price, upon which all other prices are based, can fall. This floor is the price support level. The Commodity Credit Corporation (CCC) stands ready to purchase manufactured dairy products which are the result of an oversupply engendered by the federal market order system. It is the guaranteed buyer of last resort.

Buxton and Hammond estimate only the social costs attributed to the rigidity of Class II prices. Their results are summarized in Table 5-3. They found that there was no deadweight loss when the support price was set at 75 percent of parity. This is based upon the historical observation that the CCC generally makes no purchases when the price is set at this level. Assuming that the purchased products are redistributed back to consumers, annual deadweight loss was $13 million, $65 million, and $94 million when the price support was at 80 percent, 85 percent, and 90 percent of parity, respectively. If CCC distributed its inventory abroad or destroyed it, then these estimates would be considerably higher.[15]

---

[14] Boyd M. Buxton and Jerome W. Hammond, "Social Cost of Alternative Dairy Price Support Levels," *American Journal of Agricultural Economics*, May 1974, p. 286.

[15] To the extent that these products are redistributed towards lower income groups, there may be social benefits attached to the program in terms of increased social welfare that are not subject to quantification. The same observation is true for products distributed abroad.

Table 5-3

COST ESTIMATES OF THE DAIRY PRICE
SUPPORT PROGRAM

	Percent of Parity			
	75	80	85	90
Amount support price exceeds free-market price (dollars/hundredweight)	0	0.14	0.50	0.85
Social cost (millions of dollars)				
Without distribution back to community	0	92	340	447
With distribution back to community	0	13	65	95
Transfers (millions of dollars; assuming 100 billion pounds of milk marketed)	0	140	500	850

Source: Thomas Lenard, "Government Regulation of Milk Markets Discussion Paper," prepared for the Council on Wage and Price Stability (December 1975), Table 2, p. 23. The figures presented are from Boyd M. Buxton and Jerome W. Hammond, "Social Cost of Alternative Dairy Price Support Levels," *American Journal of Agricultural Economics*, May 1974, p. 286, with the exception of transfers, which were computed by Lenard from the Buxton and Hammond data.

The deadweight loss estimates for the price support program by Buxton and Hammond can be added to the deadweight loss estimates for the federal order system by Ippolito and Masson. Ippolito and Masson used 1973 data to arrive at their estimates for the federal order system. During the market year 1973–1974, the CCC removed only 0.61 percent of total production under its purchase activities. This is a fairly small amount in absolute terms, and a much smaller figure when compared to purchases in recent years.[16] Thus, social costs attributable to the price support program were at a minimum during 1973, the year Ippolito and Masson measured social costs of the order system. The support level was set at 75 percent of parity that year; it has risen since.

It should be noted that Buxton and Hammond make no attempt to identify any loss because of rent erosion. In particular, they do not include the cost of administering the price support program, which, like the cost of administering the order system, consumes resources that could be used for other projects which have social benefits. There may, however, be some social benefits associated with the function of distributing dairy products to lower income groups domestically or

16 See Table 3-5.

abroad. Net expenditures by the CCC on the dairy support program were $496.1 million for fiscal year 1975.

Transfer Payments. There are also transfer effects generated by the price support program. In the first instance, there are transfers from the taxpaying public to the beneficiaries of the price support system, who are ultimately the producers of raw milk. Table 3-5 above contains a year-by-year summary of net expenditures by the CCC. However, these figures are not complete because the CCC inventory can be redistributed to the consuming public. A more precise measure of transfer payments has been calculated by Thomas Lenard using the figures generated by Buxton and Hammond.[17] For support levels of 80 percent, 85 percent, and 90 percent of parity, his calculations are $140 million, $500 million, and $850 million a year, respectively. These calculations are included in Table 5-3. His calculations are derived by multiplying the price rise attributed to the support system by the quantity of milk sold.

Costs of Other Regulation of Milk Marketing

Other regulation of milk marketing which generates significant social costs includes state regulation, prohibitions on the use of reconstituted milk, and import quotas on dairy products. To date, no rigorous studies of the magnitude of these costs have been completed, although some of the theoretical basis for attributing social costs to these types of regulation have been explored.[18]

Summary and Conclusions

Table 5-4 presents a generalized summary of the work of various researchers, categorized by type of regulation and type of social cost. The additional costs of price support are not included in Table 5-4. As mentioned in the introduction to this chapter, the various costs summarized are not strictly additive. In addition, the table does not reflect the results of the more recent Ippolito-Masson research that quantified the loss to grade B farmers occasioned by milk regulation. The transfer of more than $100 million away from the smaller grade

---

[17] Thomas Lenard, "Government Regulation of Milk Markets Discussion Paper," prepared for the Council on Wage and Price Stability (December 1975).

[18] The original report includes sections on state regulation, prohibitions on sale of reconstituted milk, and import quotas. Although these sections are not included here, the cost estimates presented in them are summarized in Table 5-4.

Table 5-4

SUMMARY OF SOCIAL COSTS OF MILK REGULATION AS ESTIMATED BY VARIOUS RESEARCHERS

Researcher and Category of Cost	Cost
Ippolito and Masson (1973 data)[a]	
Fluid milk price increase at retail[b]	7% (4.5 cents/gallon)
Deadweight social loss from:	
Pricing mechanism of federal orders[c]	$50 million/year
Cooperative monopolization and state regulation[d]	$70 million/year
Prohibitions on reconstitution[d]	$125 million/year[e]
Total deadweight loss	$125–$245 million/year[e]
Transfer payments from:	
Pricing mechanism of federal orders[c]	$50–$100 million/year
Cooperative monopolization[f]	$150–$200 million/year
State regulation and prohibition on reconstitution[f]	$200–$300 million/year[e]
Total transfer payments	$250–$500 million/year[e]
Kwoka (1970 data)	
Fluid milk price increase at retail[g]	22% (20.8 cents/gallon)
Total deadweight loss of regulation[h]	$202 million/year
Gross transfer payments from fluid sales[i]	$805 million/year
Roberts (1974 data)	
Potential price decrease from allowing unrestricted reconstitution of milk[j]	33 cents/gallon

a The October 1976 draft by Ippolito and Masson states a conservative figure for the cost of state plus federal regulation at about $10 million less than the January 1976 draft.

b Ippolito and Masson, "The Social Costs of Federal Regulation of Milk," p. 16.

c Ibid., p. 15.

d Ibid., n. 17.

e With what information was available, the figures on reconstituted milk are highly speculative and may represent a "best guess" of maximum possible effect.

f Ippolito and Masson, "The Social Costs of Federal Regulation of Milk," n. 18.

g John E. Kwoka, "Pricing under Federal Milk Market Regulation: Theory, Objectives, and Impact" (unpublished paper, 1975), p. 25.

h Tanya Roberts, "Review of Recent Studies," Public Interest Economics Center (1975), p. 42, summarizing Kwoka's findings.

i Ibid., p. 27.

j Ibid., p. 33.

B farmers raises additional equity questions about the impact of the regulation. Favoring one group of dairy farmers so clearly over another could hardly have been the intent of Congress.

The real value of the cost estimates is that they reflect a tangible magnitude against which any benefits of regulation can be measured. Chapter 6 takes a closer look at the results hoped for by Congress in authorizing milk regulation. The costs of regulation must be compared to the effectiveness of regulation in achieving its goals, the efficiency with which the current regulation pursues them and the continued wisdom of the original goals in the face of a completely changed market environment. This task is made easier because of the cost research that has been done. In addition, comparisons of the relative costs of various provisions can be made in order to pinpoint the costliest aspects of regulation.

6

SOCIAL BENEFITS OF
MILK REGULATION

Much has been said and written by observers of the dairy industry concerning the impact, both positive and negative, of regulation. To date, there have been no studies which have attempted to quantify the benefits attributed to the federal market order system. Nonetheless, much has been said about the benefits that the regulation was designed to secure. This chapter is not an analogue to chapter 5 which dealt with the quantitative social costs of milk regulation. Instead, benefits will simply be evaluated in terms of whether they have been achieved, and how efficient the order system has been in pursuing them. No attempt is made to place a dollar figure on any of the benefits derived from federal milk regulation. Consequently, it is impossible to make an unambiguous, dollar-for-dollar comparison of the benefits of regulation with the costs that the regulation imposes on society. However, even qualitative assessment of the benefits should be of use in determining whether and in what form milk regulation should continue.

The first step is to identify the ultimate goals of the Agricultural Adjustment Act as contained in the legislation. Congress specified four goals:

(1) Raise the income of dairy farmers.
(2) Maintain "orderly marketing conditions" such that there is an orderly flow of milk to market throughout its normal marketing season to avoid unreasonable fluctuations in supply and price.
(3) Assure an adequate and dependable supply of fluid grade milk.
(4) Prevent price levels that are either in excess of those necessary to achieve the goals of the act or those in the public interest.

Each of these goals will be discussed individually, first, by reviewing the data to see if they have in fact been achieved and, then, by analyzing the theory and the functioning of federal milk orders to determine whether they are appropriately suited to pursuing the various goals of the legislation.

Raise the Income of Dairy Farmers

Actually, Congress spoke in terms of raising the prices farmers were receiving for their product to "parity."[1] This goal has been amended in the case of milk. With regard to milk, when the secretary finds that parity prices are

> not reasonable in view of the price of feeds, the available supplies of feeds, and other economic conditions which affect market supply and demand for milk and its products in the marketing area to which the contemplated agreement, order, or amendment relates, he shall fix such prices as he finds will reflect such factors, insure a sufficient quantity of pure and wholesome milk, *and* be in the public interest.[2]

Thus, the federal milk order system is supposed to raise milk prices to a level that assures that dairy farmers' net incomes will be high enough to keep enough milk producers in business to generate a sufficient supply of pure and wholesome milk. Congress was interested in raising the income of dairy farmers, not for its own sake, but for the reason that artificially low prices could force dairy farms into premature liquidation. The lead time necessary to bring a new herd to full production can be several years. Therefore, raising producers' income is seen as a means to the end of preventing an artificial shortage caused by short-run drops in prices which result in revenues insufficient to keep a dairy farm solvent. Congress also sought to restrain price increases which were unnecessary to the achievement of the act's goals or the public interest.

Although raising prices is not equivalent to raising net income, Congress clearly intended that farmer income be raised through higher prices. In the Declaration of Conditions section of the Agricultural Adjustment Act,[3] the phrase "purchasing power of farmers" is used, connoting a concern over net income levels.

To improve producer incomes, the federal order system takes advantage of the perceived difference in price elasticity between fluid

---

[1] 7 U.S.C., section 602(1).

[2] Ibid., section 608c(18) (emphasis added).

[3] Ibid., section 601.

Table 6-1

PER CAPITA DISPOSABLE INCOME, ALL SOURCES:
FARM AS A PERCENTAGE OF NONFARM, 1960–1974

1960	1965	1970	1972	1973	1974
53.1	67.4	71.9	80.8	106.8	91.8

Source: U.S. Department of Agriculture, *Agricultural Statistics 1975* (1975), p. 464.

milk products and manufactured milk products. The higher net revenues generated from Class I sales are then dispersed among all producers of grade A milk, each thereby receiving a percentage of the increased revenues.

Has dairy farming become a more profitable enterprise because of the federal order system? Data on net income from dairy farming are not readily available. However, making subjective judgments, most observers agree that dairy farmers are not becoming rich at their occupation. Data for Indiana reveal that between 1960 and 1969 dairy farm net income rose from under $7,000 to $19,000 and the rate of return on investment went from 3.9 percent to 6.8 percent.[4] That study compared dairy farm income to crop-hog farm income and the comparison revealed that crop-hog farm incomes were much greater and much less stable. Because of the upward trend in the average size of dairy farms, it is not surprising that dairy farm income would be increasing steadily. Although the return on investment also has been increasing, the increase has not been uniform.

However, the income situation of farmers in general has shown dramatic improvement over the past fifteen years when compared to the incomes of the population at large. See Table 6-1. The per capita disposable income of the farm population has continually closed the gap so that now it is roughly equivalent to the per capita disposable income of the nonfarm population. In 1973, the per capita income of the farm population exceeded that of the nonfarm sector. Similar data are not available for dairy farmers in particular, but it is not unreasonable to infer that they too have reached a level of equivalency with the earnings of the nonfarm population.

Even so, it is not likely that the federal order system has greatly enhanced the income of dairy farmers above the general level of in-

---

[4] Ronald D. Knutson, *Cooperative Bargaining Developments in the Dairy Industry, 1960–1970*, U.S. Department of Agriculture, Farmer Cooperative Service, FCS Research Report No. 19 (August 1971), p. 28.

come in other types of farming in light of the relatively minor entry barriers to dairying. With prices fixed, production costs will rise to meet the fixed prices rather than having prices fall to reflect costs, which is what would be the result in an unregulated market. In the case of milk, costs of production will continue to escalate because of the low entry barriers and the existence of fixed factors of production. High prices and lack of significant entry barriers attract less efficient producers into the business. Fixed factors of production, which in this case means suitable dairy land, will experience capital appreciation with prices fixed at high levels.[5] This can, of course, result in windfalls to the original owners of dairy land, but does not aid the tenant farmer or the more recent purchaser of land.

The limited data on dairy farm values are consistent with the notion that the increased prices attributable to the federal order system are resulting, not in higher net incomes for dairy farmers, but in increased values of dairy farms. Some data comparing the value of all farms and dairy farms on a per acre basis are compiled in Tables 6-2 and 6-3. The per acre value of all farms rose 207 percent between 1950 and 1969. During that same period, the per acre value of dairy farms rose 217 percent. Of particular significance are the years in which dairy farms enjoyed their greatest increase in value. Although the all-farms category increased at a relatively steady rate, dairy farm increases were substantially higher between 1954 and 1959, and between 1964 and 1969. Compare this observation with the last column of Table 6-3: these higher increases coincide precisely with the years in which the percentage of all milk marketed under federal orders showed the highest increases.

Although these data suggest that fixing milk prices at artificially high levels results in at least a portion of the higher prices being capitalized in fixed assets such as land, it is impossible to assert that the regulated prices have no beneficial impact on the net income of milk producers. Reliable data simply are not available. Without data on

---

[5] This phenomenon was recognized recently by the Economic Research Service of the U.S. Department of Agriculture in a survey of dairy production costs prepared for the U.S. Senate: "If prices of agricultural products rise, land prices and rents generally rise, resulting in an increase in the total cost of production as reported here. If the cost of production were to be used to determine price supports, the increased cost would necessitate an increase in the support price. Producers, basing expectations on increased support prices, would likely further bid up land prices and rents, resulting in higher cost of production estimates. Support prices would again be adjusted upward, resulting in a never-ending cost-price spiral." U.S. Department of Agriculture, Economic Research Service, *Costs of Producing Milk in the United States, 1974*, U.S. Congress, Senate, Committee on Agriculture and Forestry, Committee Print, 94th Congress, 2d session, June 11, 1976, p. 9.

Table 6-2

VALUE PER ACRE OF FIXED ASSETS
(LAND AND BUILDINGS) IN DAIRY FARMS AND IN
ALL FARMS, 1950–1969

(dollars per acre)

	1950	1954	1959	1964	1969
Dairy farms	86.60	105.70	152.09	189.94	274.39
All farms	64.97	84.25	115.08	143.81	199.43

Source: Census of Agriculture.

Table 6-3

COMPARATIVE GROWTH IN ALL-FARM VALUE,
DAIRY FARM VALUE, AND FEDERAL MILK ORDER
REGULATION, 1950–1974

(percent)

Years	Percentage Growth in All-Farm Value	Percentage Growth in Dairy Farm Value	Growth in the Percentage of Total Milk Production Regulated by Federal Orders[a]
1950–1954	30	22	6.7
1954–1959	37	43	12.6
1959–1964	25	25	4.4
1964–1969	39	44	7.9
1969–1974	n/a	n/a	5.4

[a] The time periods covered here are actually 1950–1955, 1955–1960, 1960–1964, and 1965–1969.

Sources: Census of Agriculture; National Commission on Food Marketing, *Organization and Competition in the Dairy Industry*, Technical Study No. 3 (June 1966), p. 41; U.S. Department of Agriculture, Agricultural Marketing Service *Federal Milk Order Market Statistics, July 1975 Summary* (September 1975), p. 34.

the levels of producer income, it is also impossible to determine conclusively if the market orders have a stabilizing effect on producer incomes. There seems, however, to be a common perception that the order system does have a positive effect on producer net income, in spite of the lack of clear evidence to that effect. Nonetheless, analysis of the method employed by the order system to raise producer incomes strongly suggests that it is neither an effective, efficient, nor equitable means for achieving the goal of income enhancement.

Maintain "Orderly Marketing Conditions"

The phrase "orderly marketing conditions" is the most frequently employed phrase in all of the federal milk order literature. Its frequent use likely springs from its origin in the legislation[6] as well as from its ambiguity. In addition, orderliness has a ring of desirability; disorderliness is naturally to be disfavored. This does not mean that the phrase cannot be given a workable meaning, simply that its meaning is often not clearly enunciated. The phrase can refer to marketing conditions in the short run or in the long run, and it can refer to prices as paid by handlers, prices as received by producers, and flow of supply to market. Any of these conditions can be an aspect of "orderly marketing conditions."

Nonetheless, when *Congress* employed the term, they did so in a very limited context, namely, "an orderly flow of the supply thereof to market *through its normal marketing season* to avoid unreasonable fluctuations in supplies and prices."[7] Congress was concerned about orderly marketing in the short run, that is, on an intrayear basis. Therefore, order provisions which are based on a more expansive definition of "orderly marketing conditions" than that contained in the statute appear to be outside the ambit of the original concern of Congress in passing the legislation. Concern was expressed for intraseason price stability, production stability, and "orderly" (dependable and efficient) marketing channels for bringing milk from the farm to the table.

Prices. Stable prices are an aspect of "orderly marketing conditions." In the short run, this means a relative stability of prices during the yearly production cycle. It does not mean that there should not be a short-run seasonal variation in price to somewhat even out milk production over the marketing year, thus encouraging an orderly, or even, flow of milk year-round. However, prices have not been so flexible that fluid markets are allowed to clear during the flush season.

What then has been the behavior of prices in milk markets under the federal order system? Two prices must be examined: the prices paid by handlers and the prices received by producers. Barring a midyear amendment to a federal order, the Class I differential in each

---

[6] 7 U.S.C., section 602(4).

[7] Ibid. (emphasis added).

Figure 6-1

MONTHLY PRICES IN FEDERAL ORDER MARKETS, 1975

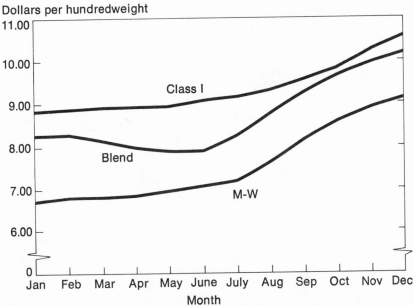

Source: U.S. Department of Agriculture, Agricultural Marketing Service, *Federal Milk Order Market Statistics, Annual Summary for 1975* (June 1976).

order remains the same throughout the entire year. Therefore, the stability of prices paid by handlers depends solely on the stability of the base price in the order, commonly the M-W price.

The stability of the prices received by the farmers, however, depends not only on the M-W price but also on the Class I utilization rate in individual orders for any given month. The blend prices received by farmers will be inherently less stable than the prices paid by handlers because the volume of milk going into Class I use is relatively stable throughout the year, while production, and the resultant rate of Class I utilization, is not. An examination of blend prices, Class I prices, and M-W prices during the past year bear this out. See Figure 6-1.

Ignoring seasonal incentive adjustments,[8] the blend prices re-

---

[8] Seasonal incentives *increase* the instability of producer prices. As of January 1, 1976, nineteen orders contained some sort of seasonal plan. U.S. Department of Agriculture, Agricultural Marketing Service, *Summary of Major Provisions in Federal Milk Market Orders, January 1, 1976* (February 1976), pp. 38–39.

Figure 6-2

PERCENTAGE INTRAYEAR VARIATION OF PRICES IN
FEDERAL MILK ORDER MARKETS, 1969–1975

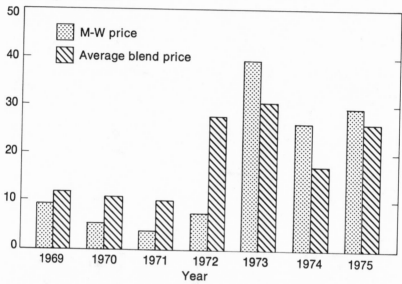

Source: U.S. Department of Agriculture, Agricultural Marketing Service, *Federal Milk Order Market Statistics*, annual summaries, 1969–1975.

ceived by producers in federal order markets during 1975 varied from 17.4 percent above the yearly average in December to 8.5 percent below the yearly average in May. This amounts to a nearly 26 percent intrayear fluctuation in monthly blend prices. In 1974, the total intrayear price fluctuation was 17.5 percent. In 1975 Class I prices fluctuated nearly 19 percent; in 1974 they fluctuated 20.5 percent.[9]

During the late 1960s and early 1970s, the M-W price fluctuated much less than the blend price under federal order markets. See Figure 6-2. In 1973, 1974, and 1975, however, the M-W price fluctuated more than order blend prices.[10] The years when the blend price fluc-

[9] U.S. Department of Agriculture, Agricultural Marketing Service, *Federal Milk Order Market Statistics, December 1975 Summary* (February 1976), p. 3 (hereinafter cited as *FMOMS*). The 1974 data suggests that the price paid by handlers fluctuates more than the price paid to producers. See discussion below.

[10] Because the M-W price is basically a competitively determined price for grade B milk in the Minnesota-Wisconsin area, the fluctuations in the M-W price can be taken as an indication of how much prices fluctuate because of seasonal variability in production.

tuated less than the M-W price may be explained in part by the fact that 1973–1975 was a highly inflationary period. The blend price cycle did not follow the usual pattern in 1973.[11] The low point was not during the spring flush but in January, and the price continued to escalate each month over the entire year, peaking in December. The M-W price went from $5.43 to $7.94 during 1973, continuing to rise to $8.15 in March 1974. Starting in April 1974, the M-W price began dropping drastically, falling steadily throughout the year to $6.41 in December.[12] Thus, in 1973 and 1974, the effects of inflation superseded the customary seasonal fluctuations. Blend prices in those two years did not follow their normal pattern either, but varied less than the M-W price.

The source of the normal, cyclical variability of the blend price is the difference between Class I and Class II prices. The greater the differential, the more the blend price will fluctuate, given a constant fluctuation in the utilization rate. Narrowing the differential would increase the stability of prices received by the farmers, although this would be correctly perceived by producers as lowering the average price they receive over the year. Thus, it can be said that the federal order system sacrifices producer price stability to some extent in favor of a higher average price over the course of the year if it is true that the Class I differentials could be lower and still consistent with the goals of the legislation. The advantage of the present regulated price structure, in which producer prices fluctuate even more than would be the case in a free market, is that it should encourage more level production year-round. Seasonal incentive payment plans amplify this effect.

A general conclusion about the pricing mechanism under federal orders is that they really are not particularly well adapted to stabilizing producer prices. Rather, it is the prices paid by handlers that are stabilized by the federal orders since the differentials for the various use classes are fixed. The prices can be no more stable than the M-W price, an arguably free-market price, allows them to be. Still, as a general rule, handler prices are more stable than producer prices. This is a curious result in light of the overriding theme of the legislation which was to provide stability for farmers. This observation suggests that price stability itself is not of great importance to farmers so long

---

[11] The usual cycle for blend price is to rise in the fall, gradually drop to a low point in the late spring or early summer, and rise to a high point again in the fall.

[12] U.S. Department of Agriculture, FMOMS, *Annual Summary for 1973* (June 1974); FMOMS, *Annual Summary for 1974* (June 1975).

Table 6-4

PERCENTAGE INTRAYEAR VARIABILITY OF MILK PRICES IN
SIX MARKETS, SELECTED PREORDER YEARS

Market	1920	1924	1928
New England	21.1	39.8	30.1
New York	28.7	42.5	31.2
Philadelphia	23.8	7.5	6.6
Baltimore	19.2	10.8	11.2[a]
Cincinnati	21.4	61.1	19.4
Minneapolis-St. Paul	42.1	32.1	8.7
Simple average	26.1	32.3	17.9

[a] Denotes 1927 data.

Source: Hutzel Metzger, *Cooperative Marketing of Fluid Milk,* U.S. Department of Agriculture, Technical Bulletin No. 179 (May 1930), pp. 88–90.

as the fluctuation is predictable. One further comparison will bear this out.

Table 6-4 contains a summary of prices received by producers who marketed their milk through cooperative associations in six metropolitan areas during three preorder years: 1920, 1924, and 1928. The yearly percentage fluctuations in producer prices month-to-month vary between 42.5 percent and 6.6 percent. The simple average fluctuation over all the markets for all three years was 25.4 percent.[13] Fluctuations in blend prices in federal orders during the late 1960s and early 1970s were considerably less than these 1920s figures. However, blend price fluctuation during the mid-1970s is roughly equivalent to the level of fluctuation during the 1920s.[14] Based on this comparison, it cannot be said that the federal order system has contributed unequivocally to price stability from the producer's standpoint. It is unlikely that the level of price fluctuation is as important to the farmer as its predictability. Price fluctuation is not now remarkably different from the preorder days. What may be different is the source of the fluctuation and its predictability.

During the years covered by Table 6-4, price fluctuations were largely a result of the necessarily local markets for raw milk and the one-sided bargaining relationship between farmers and dairies. Now the level of variability comes from the regulatory scheme, a pro-

[13] Hutzel Metzger, *Cooperative Marketing of Fluid Milk,* U.S. Department of Agriculture, Technical Bulletin No. 179 (May 1930), pp. 88–90.
[14] Compare Figure 6–2 with Table 6–4.

grammed variability. The former type was what concerned Congress. The variation during the 1920s resulted from lockouts by dairies, poor transaction technology, the comparative nonexistence of effective cooperatives, and, later, contracting demand caused by the Depression. These conditions no longer prevail. The similar magnitude of price fluctuation still existing today is more palatable to farmers because its source is known and can be planned for.

It is significant that the source of the instability that concerned Congress would no longer exist, with or without regulation. Farmers are no longer at the mercy of local buyers as milk markets have, as a technological matter, reached regional proportions. Without price regulation, most markets would experience a level of fluctuation similar to that currently encountered, and in all markets the fluctuation would be predictable. Such fluctuations would simply be the result of the well-known supply/demand variations that occur intrayear. In light of the technological developments, it is not surprising that price stability to farmers has been deemphasized in the administration of the order system.

Production and Flow to Market. Orderly marketing conditions in the short run also mean stability of both production and flow to market. Given the nature of the dairy industry, the goals of stable flow to market and stability of prices, as discussed above, present an inherent conflict. Dairy cows are simply more productive in the spring than in the fall. In order to encourage a stability of flow to market, which would only result from stable production, given the perishable nature of the fluid product, some degree of price incentive must be present. Seasonal incentive plans are designed to help create this price incentive in the context of the order system.

What has been the history of the production/consumption cycles in federal milk markets? Tables 6-5 and 6-6 summarize data on total monthly production and monthly production going into Class I for recent years. These tables show that production in federal order markets peaks in May and hits a low point sometime during the fall, usually October or November. The monthly production, as measured by producer deliveries to regulated handlers, generally varies about 20 percent intrayear. Deliveries used in Class I vary intrayear in the vicinity of 15 percent. However, the maximum volume of milk going into Class I generally occurs in the fall, frequently October. The least amount of milk going into Class I usually occurs in June or July. Thus, the fluid bottling/consumption cycle is almost perfectly countercyclical to the raw milk production cycle. As an example, Figure 6-3 shows the fluid consumption and raw milk production cycles for 1975.

Table 6-5

VARIABILITY OF THE VOLUME OF PRODUCER MILK MARKETED UNDER FEDERAL ORDERS, 1965–1975

(volume in millions of pounds)

Year	High		Low		Monthly Average	Percentage Variation from Average
	Month	Volume	Month	Volume		
1975	May	6,502	February	5,298	5,771	20.9
1974	May	6,333	February	5,082	5,648	22.1
1973	May	6,270	November	4,983	5,518	23.3
1972	May	6,415	November	5,163	5,727	21.9
1971	May	6,274	February	5,143	5,642	20.0
1970	May	6,042	February	4,939	5,413	20.4
1969	May	5,737	November	4,759	5,086	19.2
1968	May	5,190	February	4,492	4,704	10.3
1967	May	5,010	September	4,165	4,476	18.9
1966	May	4,926	November	4,031	4,418	20.3
1965	May	5,162	September	4,160	4,537	22.1

Source: U.S. Department of Agriculture, *Federal Milk Order Market Statistics*, annual summaries, 1965–1975.

Table 6-6

VARIABILITY OF THE VOLUME OF PRODUCER MILK USED IN CLASS I PRODUCTS, 1965–1975

(volume in millions of pounds)

Year	High		Low		Monthly Average	Percentage Variation from Average
	Month	Volume	Month	Volume		
1975	October	3,635	February	3,173	3,342	13.8
1974	October	3,538	June	2,922	3,274	18.8
1973	March	3,666	July	3,126	3,377	16.0
1972	October	3,597	July	3,109	3,411	14.3
1971	March	3,530	June	3,043	3,343	14.6
1970	October	3,607	June	3,072	3,328	16.1
1969	October	3,552	June	2,953	3,264	18.4
1968	October	3,414	June	2,590	3,041	27.1
1967	March	3,027	July	2,615	2,867	14.4
1966	March	3,129	June	2,677	2,900	15.6
1965	October	3,051	June	2,679	2,880	12.9

Source: U.S. Department of Agriculture, *Federal Milk Order Market Statistics*, annual summaries, 1965–1975.

125

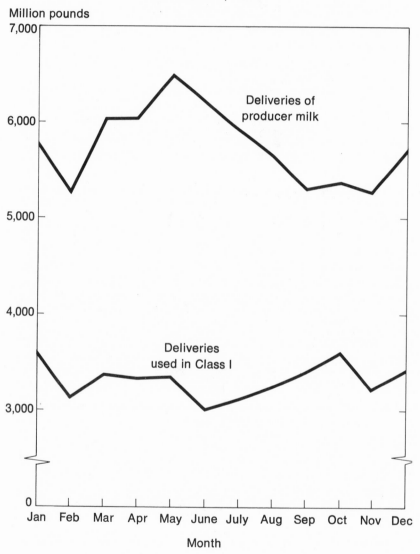

Figure 6-3

VOLUME OF PRODUCER MILK DELIVERED TO HANDLERS
REGULATED UNDER FEDERAL MILK ORDERS AND VOLUME
OF PRODUCER MILK USED FOR CLASS I PRODUCTS,
BY MONTH, 1975

Million pounds

Deliveries of producer milk

Deliveries used in Class I

Month

Source: U.S. Department of Agriculture, Agriculture Marketing Service,
Federal Milk Order Market Statistics, Annual Summary for 1975, pp. 33 and 41.

To date, the technology and government regulation of milk marketing has not advanced to the state that the production cycle matches the demand cycle for Class I products. It is highly improbable that it ever will. Although improving technology has much to offer in the way of stabilizing milk production, the government still finds itself in a quandary as to its proper role. There continues to be a significant trade-off between stable prices and stable production. If regulation is to encourage stable production and flow to market, it must do so by offering price incentives during the low production months. If this is done, prices are necessarily less stable, although not less predictable.

Still, production variability does seem to be less today than in preorder times, at least in some regions. During the 1920s, some milksheds had variations approaching 75 percent or more, although in others it was less than 25 percent.[15] However, it cannot be said that productions would not have stabilized anyway simply because of technological advances and the geographical expansion of markets.

Conclusions. The results of the federal order system in achieving "orderly marketing conditions" as that term was defined *by the legislation*,[16] have been somewhat equivocal. Available evidence shows that prices to producers are not appreciably more stable now than under preorder conditions. Increased stability of production seems to have been advanced to some extent, but not to the point where it matches the demand cycle. Furthermore, stability of production has been achieved only at the expense of stable producer prices and the insulation of local markets from outside competition.

In several respects, federal milk orders are ill-designed for achieving some of the characteristics of "orderly markets" which they were intended to pursue. As with the income enhancement objective, the shortcomings that exist ultimately flow from the mechanism of classified and blend prices. This is particularly true where the stabilization of producer prices is concerned.

---

[15] Metzger, *Cooperative Marketing of Fluid Milk*, p. 29.

[16] A "corollary" of orderly marketing was advanced in Milk Pricing Advisory Committee, *The Milk Pricing Problem*, Report to the U.S. Department of Agriculture, Part I (March 1972), p. 4: "Orderliness implies short-term protection of a market from unwarranted movement of milk supplies." Although the term "unwarranted" is not defined by the committee, presumably it would mean at least that local pools should not be "loaded" with milk of distant production regions if not needed. In reality, this has happened frequently. The committee specifically rejects the notion that protection of local markets from unwarranted milk movements means that the local markets should be insulated from competition. The report goes on to say (p. 4) that orderly marketing connotes "adjustment of supply to least cost sources as well as to regional changes in production costs." Nonetheless, federal order market provisions discriminate severely against interorder shipments of milk.

The price received by the milk producer is the blend price. This price depends upon the Class I utilization rate in the market for a previous month.[17] These monthly utilization rates are fairly unstable because of the countercyclical timing of demand for Class I products and total raw milk production. In 1975 the Class I utilization was 49 percent in June; it was 66 percent in October, a substantial variation.[18] This contributes to the instability of the blend price, which normally fluctuates more than the M-W price.[19] (Recall that the M-W price is the competitively determined base price upon which the price structure of the federal order system depends.)

The large variability in blend prices arises not so much from classified pricing itself, but because the Class I differential is so large. The size of the Class I differential affects the impact of a changing utilization rate upon the blend price. In the extreme case, if the Class I differential were zero, changing utilization rates would have no effect upon the blend price, assuming there was some Class II milk in the market. As the Class I differential increases, the variability of the blend price increases. This effect strongly suggests that the current class prices are not set for the purpose of stabilizing prices, but rather for some other reasons, possibly to include increasing producer returns. If that is the case, Class I prices will more nearly reflect what the market will bear.

In addition to creating instability problems, this pricing philosophy creates problems of diminishing Class I profits because of overproduction. These problems evoke a response on the part of milk producers to raise the Class I differential, with hopes of exploiting the more protected fluid market. Some pressure may be brought to bear on the USDA to increase the regulated Class I differential. However, cooperatives commonly respond to demand by their members for higher returns by charging over-order premiums. These premiums further increase price instability to the cooperatives' members and encourage more production.

These observations on price instability ignore completely the added fluctuations caused by the operation of the seasonal incentive plans in use in many of the orders. These plans are used to encourage added production in the shortage months by raising prices even higher during the time they are normally highest and lowering prices during the months when they are normally at their lowest. Producer accept-

---

[17] The prices for the *next* month are announced in the middle of each month, and are based on the M-W price for the *previous* month.

[18] U.S. Department of Agriculture, *FMOMS, Annual Summary for 1975* (June 1976), p. 45.

[19] See Figure 6–2.

ance of these programs and policies which increase price fluctuation suggests that, as a group, they prefer pricing policies based upon the goal of increasing average prices for the year rather than stabilizing prices throughout the year.

If price stability is to be retained as a goal of the federal order system, and if classified pricing is to be retained, then more stability could be achieved by narrowing the price difference between fluid and surplus class milk. The Class I price could be lowered, which would yield a higher Class II price, yielding a blend price that would still draw forth the amount of fluid grade milk deemed necessary to supply fluid needs adequately. Resulting blend prices would be lower than those in effect now, but only because they are now at levels which bring forth surplus grade A milk in excessive quantities.

With respect to encouraging an orderly flow of product to market on an intrayear basis, the classified/blend price mechanism is conceptually consistent with this goal. It allows price incentives to exist for producers to even out their production. Blend prices, dependent upon utilization rates, will rise during the fall and decline during the spring. This fact is well known and anticipated by milk producers, although the lag built into the order system pricing mechanism creates a slight distortion. In practice, however, the flexibility of the blend price has still been deemed inadequate in many markets and the seasonal incentive plans have been instituted. These plans further increase the price variability with the objective of even greater incentives for smoothing out monthly production. It is ironic that price stability is still claimed as a goal of regulation. Blend prices already vary more than the M-W price, and then additional regulations are superimposed to increase the seasonal fluctuations which resemble those said to characterize the "disorderly" conditions of an unregulated market.

An additional aspect of orderly flow to market—one to which the system is no longer well adapted—is that all the milk produced can be efficiently marketed through known channels before it spoils. Advancing technology has increased the ability to both store and transport raw milk so that greater choices are open to the milk producer in marketing his milk. The individual farmer now has vast amounts of information available to him to help make intelligent marketing decisions. Cooperatives play a vital role in disseminating market information to members. Modern communication technology has eliminated the spector of the milk producer being turned away at the dairy door without alternative buyers of his milk. To the extent that orderly marketing means the efficient bringing together of buyers and sellers before spoilage, the classified/blend price mechanism no longer makes much of a contribution in light of current transaction technology. Instead, the order system creates the marketing problem of disposing of surplus milk at artificially lower prices, and it erects barriers to the production and sale of reconstituted milk products, thereby eliminating the potential for whatever stabilizing influences a storable milk product would have.

The local bias of the order system, which is implemented by offering all producers a "Florida-minus-transport" price for their milk also impedes the ability of local markets to gravitate toward those supply regions that can most economically provide them milk. Efficient production regions have less incentive to sell in the less efficient markets if they can get the equivalent price locally. With markets artificially localized, farmers are currently unable to take advantage of the potential vast expansion of possible outlets brought about by improved storage, transport, and communications technology. Raw milk is unique among farm commodities in that the marketing of it is currently not aided by a brokerage system. This is largely because of the local market bias contained in the federal order system, a holdover from the 1930s when the technology of milk marketing made all milk markets local by necessity. Although this is no longer the case, federal regulation has nevertheless "locked in" the marketing system of the Depression by requiring that markets be served by local producers. This local bias has resulted in the benefits of modern marketing technology being lost to consumers of milk.

Assure an Adequate and Dependable Supply of Fluid Grade Milk

Where "orderly marketing" capsulizes the original intent of the statute in the area of short-run objectives, this goal reflects one of the prime long-run concerns of Congress. The adequate supply goal was not part of the original act, which was perceived as a short-run emergency measure, but was added in the 1937 amendments to the act.

The term "adequate supply" means simply that, in the long run, prices to farmers will be at a level which will assure continued productive capacity sufficient to meet the demand for *fluid* milk. The price level in the federal order system is directed toward this goal, and the goal is successfully achieved because the quantity of fluid milk demanded is artificially suppressed as a result of the enhanced Class I prices. In a sense, the classified/blend price mechanism is self-fulfilling in terms of the adequate supply goal. By raising the price of Class I milk, the federal order system guarantees that less milk will be demanded for fluid use. The higher the Class I price, the lower the volume of Class I milk demanded. The lower the Class I demand, the easier it is for producers to come forward with what can be called an adequate supply.

The size of the surplus (that amount of grade A production in excess of the fluid milk consumed) deemed adequate is a question that can only be answered by reference to the current technology of fluid milk bottling. Although opinions differ, many experts in dairy marketing have suggested that a 20 percent surplus is necessary in order for the supply to be "adequate."[20] In 1975, the utilization rate for all federal orders combined was 58 percent, which means that the surplus amounted to 72 percent of actual Class I usage. This far exceeds the 20 percent estimate.[21] Currently, each order market must be primarily responsible for generating its own surplus because of the way order provisions localize markets. If larger geographic areas were involved, the surplus necessary could very well be reduced. The trend toward fewer, larger federal orders may prove beneficial in this respect. Still, the question about supply is not whether the surplus is adequate, but whether it is chronically excessive. Most observers maintain that it is the latter.[22]

Because the goals of the federal order system need to be balanced, the goal of "adequate supply" must be harmonized with the other stated goals which have not been as strongly emphasized. This is particularly so with regard to the fourth goal, the prevention of excessive prices, since oversupply occurs as a result of setting price levels higher than necessary to encourage only the volume of grade A production actually needed.

---

[20] See, for example, Charles Bartlett, "Bringing Federal Order Pricing Up to Date and in Line with Antitrust Regulations," *Illinois Agricultural Economics* (June 1974), p. 7; Hugh L. Cook et al., *Review of Eisenstadt, Philip, Robert T. Masson, and David Roddy, "An Economic Analysis of the Associated Milk Producers, Inc., Monopoly,"* Research Bulletin R2790 (Madison: University of Wisconsin, January 1976), p. 11.

[21] See U.S. Department of Agriculture, *FMOMS, Annual Summary for 1975*, pp. 44–45, which presents a map depicting grade A surpluses in federal orders by region. The vast majority of federal orders each had considerably more than the 20 percent surplus deemed necessary.

[22] The seriousness of the oversupply problem has reached the point where there has actually been some call for supply controls. According to the Milk Pricing Advisory Committee, "supply control can be used to raise producer returns by overcoming the tendency of the industry to chronically generate excess supplies. If applied in a more stringent manner, it can be used to enhance producer returns substantially. The more stringently applied, the more restrictions must be placed on the freedom of new producers to enter the industry and on the normal tendency of existing producers to respond to higher milk prices." Milk Pricing Advisory Committee, *The Milk Pricing Problem*, Part I, p. 14. Such an anticompetitive step was certainly not contemplated by the original enactment. Further, the "tendency" to generate excess supplies is not a characteristic of the industry, but rather a result of the regulation of the industry.

Part of the reason that Class I differentials have become so large is the inability of the federal order system to generate the higher net incomes which producers expect of it. The solution to this failure is erroneously perceived to be to increase further the Class I differentials, either through cooperative premiums or through the USDA, for the purpose of improving blend prices. This solution leads to further overproduction, resulting in continued disruptive pressures. The remaining reason for high Class I differentials flows from the "Florida-minus-transport" pricing policy. Florida is among the most ill-suited regions of the country for dairying, so prices there must be set at the highest levels in order to provide local production. In order to prevent milk from being shipped to Florida from more efficient areas in order to draw the higher prices, the federal order prices for Class I milk diminish only by the approximated cost of transporting bulk milk to Florida. In most northern markets, the gains in efficiency outstrip the more modest transport decreases, resulting in higher-than-necessary prices in northern markets which generate the overproduction characteristic of the order system. Milk will still not be shipped south since the high prices are also available in the north. Thus, every time a more inefficient area is incorporated into the order system, it may become necessary to increase local prices all the way back to the Minnesota-Wisconsin area to prevent flows of producer milk south. Federal regulation in Florida increased substantially in 1966 and 1967 with the additions of the Tampa Bay and Upper Florida orders.[23] In 1967, the Class I differential in the Minneapolis-St. Paul order was 76 cents, going up to 86 cents in 1968, and $1.06 in 1969.[24] Higher prices in the productive regions are necessary if Florida is to be supplied by Florida producers. Adequate supplies in Florida are accomplished only by having chronic oversupply in other areas as a result of excessive Class I prices.

This method of assuring an adequate supply quickly loses touch with the reason why an adequate supply of fluid grade milk is sought. It is not because surplus milk is desirable of itself, but because milk is considered a basic food that should be available for consumption. The current system has reached the point where it is analogous to a law simply stating that only half of all fluid grade milk produced may be processed for consumption; the rest must be kept off the market as constant proof of adequate supply. To the extent that the adequate supply goal of the Agricultural Adjustment Act discloses a policy favoring the consumption of fluid milk, the federal order system, be-

---

[23] U.S. Department of Agriculture, FMOMS, Annual Summary for 1975, p. 8.
[24] U.S. Department of Agriculture, Summary of Major Provisions in Federal Milk Marketing Orders, January 1, 1967, pp. 52–53; and U.S. Department of Agriculture, FMOMS, Annual Summary for 1969 (June 1970), p. 56.

cause of its price structure, has become self-defeating by pricing potential fluid milk consumers out of the market.

Prevent Excessive Prices

For purposes of this section, a price that is in excess of that necessary to achieve the goals of the Agricultural Adjustment Act will be referred to as an "unduly enhanced" price. Although the phraseology of "undue price enhancement" is borrowed from the Capper-Volstead Act,[25] the same imperative appears in somewhat different language in the Agricultural Adjustment Act. The secretary shall authorize "no action under this chapter which has for its purpose the maintenance of prices to farmers above the level which it is declared to be the policy of Congress to establish in subsection (1) of this section."[26] Originally, it was the policy of Congress to establish parity prices for milk but this policy was amended in 1937. In the case of milk, the secretary is to first determine parity prices for milk, and then adjust them to "reflect the price of feeds, the available supplies of feeds, and other economic conditions which affect market supply and demand for milk, . . . insure a sufficient quantity of pure and wholesome milk, *and* be in the public interest."[27] If prices as set by the secretary are maintained above those that either reflect the various economic factors, or insure a sufficient quantity of milk, or are in the public interest, then those prices are greater than the prices declared to be the policy of the act and therefore are unlawful. The price level must be consistent with *all* of these guidelines.

There are two potential sources of undue price enhancement. The first is simply that the minimum prices set by the secretary are too high. The second source is the administration of the order system in a manner which allows local milk monopolies to develop and create undue price enhancement through the extraction of monopolistic over-order premiums. Since the legislation admonishes the secretary to authorize "no action under this chapter" which has for its purpose the maintenance of unduly high prices, administration of the order system in a manner that allows local monopolies to exist and raise prices is condemned as much as setting order prices too high.[28] There was

---

[25] 7 U.S.C., section 292.

[26] Ibid., section 602(2)b.

[27] Ibid., section 608c(18) (emphasis added).

[28] The Federal Milk Order Study (Nourse) Committee is in accord. A goal of the order system is to "attain reasonable competition but not local monopoly resulting in undue price enhancement." Edwin G. Nourse et al., *Report to the Secretary of Agriculture by the Federal Milk Order Study Committee*, U.S. Department of Agriculture (December 1962), p. 13.

considerable discussion of the discontinuation of orders if producers were able to extract prices in excess of those declared to be the policy of the act. In essence, it was the understanding of members of Congress that such a situation demonstrated that the order was no longer needed.[29]

When are prices unduly enhanced? When prices are at a level above that level which is declared to be the policy of the act. That level is a price which will insure a sufficient quantity of grade A milk. If prices prevail above that level, they are unduly enhanced. In light of the chronic surpluses of grade A milk existing in most federal order regions, the conclusion is inescapable that these supplies are only called forth because of higher-than-necessary prices.

In terms of results, it matters little whether undue price enhancement is in the form of minimum order prices that are too high or in the form of over-order premiums extracted by monopolistic cooperatives. Either source of undue price enhancement would result in the chronic surpluses of grade A milk that have become characteristic of most federal order markets.

Although the naked existence of unnecessary supplies (72 percent in 1975) is the most unequivocal evidence of prices being too high, additional factors support this conclusion and suggest that the source of the undue price enhancement results both from the minimums set by the Department of Agriculture and also from over-order premiums collected by cooperatives.

First, the process by which minimum prices are set suggests that they are set too high. Although the statute requires that prices be set based upon the conditions that prevail in each milk marketing order region,[30] the secretary has essentially abandoned this as the primary consideration.[31] Instead, the price-setting mechanism has been based

---

[29] See 7 U.S.C., section 608c(16)(A), which requires that an order be terminated whenever the secretary finds that it does not tend to effectuate the declared policy of the act.

[30] Ibid., section 608c(18).

[31] "In the past, milk orders have generally been tailored to individual local milk markets. In recent years, however, the procurement and marketing of milk and dairy products have become more regional and national in scope. Consequently, markets for milk have become much broader in scope. This is reflected in the size of marketing areas where milk is regulated by a single order. Some of these areas encompass whole States and even territory in several States. The flow of milk from farm to consumer, however, may extend even beyond the boundaries of these broader areas. For that reason, a change in one order—particularly a change in price—affects supply-demand balance in other markets unless related changes are made in the other orders. Many of today's marketing problems must be viewed in the perspective of the national milk supply and the total demand for milk in the country." U.S. Department of Agriculture, Agricultural Marketing Service, *Questions and Answers on Federal Milk Marketing Orders* (March 1975), p. 13.

more heavily on regional and national price alignment calculated to assure all areas local production, at the expense of massive over-production in most areas. In practice, prices are set to align from the midwestern milkshed to the southern markets, based roughly upon the distance the individual orders are from the milkshed. Proponents of the order system argue this approach is necessary to prevent "artificial" flow of producer milk in and out of local market orders. Critics perceive it as a form of pricing to limit entry into the market. The report of the Milk Pricing Advisory Committee concluded:

> When markets were local in character, considerable weight was given to local supply-demand conditions in applying the pricing standards. But as procurement and distribution areas have grown and fluid milk markets became regional in nature, more weight has been given to regional and national supply-demand factors. Increasingly, it will be necessary to give primary consideration to national supply-demand conditions in applying the pricing standard. This is not to say that adjustment of individual market prices may not be necessary from time to time *to achieve proper alignment of Class I and blend prices between markets.*[32]

The alignment referred to is the "Florida-minus-transport" prices that emanate, from Eau Claire, Wisconsin, the basing point. Whenever Class I price alignment results in prices in local markets that call forth heavy overproduction, undue price enhancement results. The fact of overproduction, taken together with the allocation provisions in each order which discourage the interorder flow of raw milk, suggests that there is undue price enhancement *as a result* of the minimum prices set by the Department of Agriculture.

The second source of undue price enhancement results from co-operative control of milk supplies. Such enhancement is suggested by over-order premiums charged by local cooperatives, and it is in addition to any undue price enhancement flowing from minimum prices being set too high by the individual orders. The mere existence of an over-order premium does not necessarily mean that there is undue price enhancement as contemplated by the Congress. Short-run supply deficiencies in some markets might well result in higher prices, as the federal order prices are not designed to respond rapidly to sudden deficiencies.

However, over-order premiums based upon a bona fide shortage of supply would have two characteristics. The first would be that the over-order charges would be fairly temporary in nature, with more

---

[32] Milk Pricing Advisory Committee, *The Milk Pricing Problem*, Part I, p. 9 (emphasis added).

distant producers, especially those delivering to markets with lower Class I utilizations, reacting to the higher prices by meeting demand within a short-run period. The other characteristic of a bona fide shortage would be that premiums are charged for *all* classes of milk. A cooperative selling Class I milk with a premium and at the same time selling Class II or III milk at a lower or nonpremium price is inconsistent with the notion of a bona fide shortage.[33] If a real shortage existed, no one would be willing to sell raw milk for a manufacturing class price less than that price available from fluid-use handlers. Therefore, whenever over-order premiums are of lengthy duration or apply only to Class I products, it is highly unlikely that the over-order charges are anything other than undue price enhancement resulting from monopoly control.

One further caveat relative to over-order charges: There can be greater costs associated with servicing Class I buyers. If that were the case, the service charge would be assessed against *all* milk delivered to fluid bottlers instead of against only that milk ultimately classified as Class I. This is simply because the additional costs, if any, are incurred by the cooperative in delivering suitable Class I product to the dairy, whether the dairy ultimately uses it for that purpose or not.

Thus, the key indications of market power are the differences in premiums between Class I and Class II sales, and the differences between Class I and Class II service charges to predominantly fluid bottlers. In addition, it should be noted that if a cooperative is operating some sort of base-surplus plan for paying its members, then the cooperative is seeking to restrict production, and that behavior is inconsistent with a bona fide shortage of milk. If a cooperative is both charging premiums and at the same time operating a base-surplus plan, there is a strong suggestion that the premiums are monopolistic.

The history of over-order premiums indicates that they do exist over time in markets where there is no shortage, and that they have been overwhelmingly applied to Class I sales both in incidence and in amount. Although the magnitudes have varied, premiums have existed in all major regions of the country. Moreover, a correlation exists between market share and the amount of over-order charges. There is less than one chance in ten thousand that the premium/market share pattern that exists would exist by mere happenstance. The prices that result because of the existence of a causal relationship between market share and premium level would constitute undue price enhancement within the meaning of the act. This is because it would

---

[33] Replies to the questionnaire of the Department of Justice to selected cooperatives reveal that over-order premiums are overwhelmingly applied, both in incidence and in amount, to Class I sales.

be derived from the exercise of market power rather than from a bona fide shortage.

Summary and Conclusions

Chapter 5 reviewed estimates of the costs of milk regulation as compared to an unregulated market. Historically, the costs associated with regulation were intended to "buy" certain benefits, most notably, assurance that a fluid milk shortage would not develop because of artificially depressed prices causing premature exits from dairy farming. Sufficient supplies were to be assured, without undue price enhancement, by establishing orderly short-run marketing conditions and by raising milk producer income. Instead, through a combination of seeking to exploit differences in demand for different dairy products and attempting to preserve a localized marketing system in the face of increased technological advances toward national markets for milk, the order system has caused or contributed to the following results:

(1) Price levels in many markets, particularly in the more efficient production regions, that bring forth chronic oversupplies of grade A milk. Such price levels constitute excessive prices as condemned by the act.

(2) Inefficient, inequitable, and regressive attempts to raise producer incomes through the classified/blend pricing mechanism.

(3) Accentuated fluctuations, in the prices received by farmers because of the higher-than-necessary Class I differentials which reflect a "Florida-minus-transport" pricing policy of reflecting differences in costs of production between grade A and grade B milk.

(4) Artificial localization of supply areas through pricing and allocation provisions.

(5) Facilitation of undesirable behavior on the part of dairy cooperatives, resulting in monopolistic pricing.

In view of these undesirable effects and side effects of milk regulation, it would be somewhat premature to attempt to balance the costs of regulation with the benefits regulation is intended to secure until and unless the actual results of the system are brought more nearly in line with the goals of the legislation. Chapter 7 looks at some of the possible means for accomplishing this. It also examines alternatives to the present system which recognize that the original goals of Congress are outmoded.

7

SUMMARY OBSERVATIONS
AND POSSIBLE REMEDIES

The purpose of this report is to assess the competitive impact of federal milk market orders, the conduct of dairy cooperatives, and the interaction of the two. The analysis proceeded on the assumption that too little attention has been focused on the competitive impact and the continued need for extensive economic regulation of milk marketing. As a foundation for this analysis, the legislative and general history of the dairy industry at the time of the enactment of the Capper-Volstead Act and the Agricultural Adjustment Act are reviewed. This review is important both in understanding Congress' intent in enacting the legislation and in determining its success. Federal milk orders are then analyzed to determine the current effects of their various provisions. In addition, the type of conduct engaged in by dairy cooperatives within the order system is outlined. Finally, quantitative estimates of the costs of regulation are reviewed, and the results of the system are compared with the benefits sought by Congress.

There are several readily apparent observations that can be made based on this analysis. First, there is a startling contrast between milk marketing in the 1920s and 1930s (or 1950s) and milk marketing today. Where milk markets were once inherently local because of technology, they are now kept local by regulation in spite of technology. Markets that were of necessity highly local in character had many small producers who were typically unorganized, facing few handlers. They have been replaced by markets of substantially greater size, wherein producers are represented by highly effective bargaining cooperatives and federations and typically have multiple outlets for their milk. Further, the current communication and information-gathering capabilities bear little comparison with such capabilities in the 1920s and 1930s. Such contrasts alone should call into question the continuing need for the federal market orders, as well as raising issues about the proper scope of the antitrust immunity granted cooperatives.

A further observation, however, makes the need for reassessment of federal regulation of milk marketing even more imperative: federal milk orders are a significant deviation from a free-market economy, which deviation creates substantial undesirable economic effects. The system as administered has succeeded to a startling extent in maintaining milk markets as they existed in the 1930s. Of course, markets are larger today, and the participants, particularly cooperatives, are changed. The goal of an adequate supply for local consumption needs has been achieved; however, the need frequently is inappropriately supplied from local production, to the substantial detriment of consumers and some producers. Consumers have been denied certain product choices (at a price reflecting their real cost), and they have suffered lowered consumption of fluid milk products because of artificially high prices set by the order system. Dairy farmers have not received the "benefits" of the regulation in an equitable manner, and markets have been artificially foreclosed to efficient producers. The most substantial problem that results from the order system is the persistent and overwhelming surplus of grade A milk production. This result of the order system alone raises serious questions about the need for, and the administration of, the orders.

The federal order system does not operate in a vacuum. A further conclusion that flows from the analysis of the report is that federal order regulation has been instrumental in the achievement and maintenance of market power by dairy cooperatives. Absent the federal order system, monopolization of local markets would be less likely. However, by creating a bias for local market production (barriers for nonlocal milk), the order system increases the potential for monopolization. In many markets, cooperatives have taken steps to realize that potential. As Congress predicted, control of production output in an agricultural product like milk is not possible. What is possible under the federal order system is control of the eligible Class I milk supply in an order market. Through mergers, federations, full-supply contracts, pool loading, operation of standby pools, and operation of "surplus balancing" plants, some dairy cooperatives have isolated their orders from alternative sources of Class I eligible milk, and they have controlled the surplus Class I eligible milk within their order markets. The ultimate goal is increased revenues, realized through monopolistic over-order charges extracted from handlers with insufficient alternative sources of milk supply.

The quantitative analysis of the costs of the current system of milk marketing contrasted with the qualitative analysis of the purported benefits of the system suggest several observations in the nature of questions. One is whether the goals as outlined by Congress still require massive regulation in order to be realized. The order system has evolved into a generally inefficient and ineffective means of achieving the broadly outlined congressional goals. The order system and cooperative monopolization have cost consumers and society millions of dollars each year in overcharges, deadweight losses, and transfer payments. Some farmers (grade B and Minnesota and Wisconsin grade A) actually lose income to other farmers (all other grade A). It is difficult to imagine that Congress intended this result. This observation together with others made about the undesirable effects of the order system (for example, chronic oversupplies of grade A milk) provide additional reason for administrative and congressional reevaluation of federal milk marketing regulation.

Finally, there are some summary observations about the impact of the current system on consumers, handlers, or milk producers. Consumers are harmed by high prices, lowered fluid consumption, and restricted product choices. Handlers are harmed by the elimination of opportunities to compete in supply procurement and artificial limitations on the products they can market and the suppliers with whom they can reasonably deal. The system is not in the best interest of dairy farmers because not all of the benefits intended for them by Congress have been realized, and what benefits there are have been bestowed in an inequitable or regressive fashion.

This report does not propose to have the final answers to the questions raised by its observations. There are, however, some possible remedies to the problems identified by the report that can be suggested.

Reducing Class I Differentials

The congressional mandate to maintain "orderly marketing conditions" can be fulfilled at a lower cost to society with only minor administrative changes in the federal order system. When the secretary of agriculture determines the appropriate price of milk for an order, he makes a determination that the price he arrives at is a price sufficient to call forth an adequate supply of pure and wholesome milk and is in the public interest. The term "adequate supply" has never been fully defined, but it certainly means something to the effect that there will be a sufficient amount of milk available for buyers to consume in fluid form at reasonable prices.

Assuming, for the sake of argument, that the current system of regulation achieves this goal, then exactly the same form of regulation, but with *smaller* fluid differentials, would effectuate the purposes of the act equally well and at a lower cost to society. This would be accomplished by eliminating the implicit requirement that each market must have an adequate supply of locally produced milk to satisfy its fluid needs. Massive surpluses of milk exist in the Chicago order as well as several other milk orders, and milk from the Upper Midwest has a demonstrated ability to be shipped from the Upper Midwest to markets in Florida, despite the barriers to interorder milk movement imposed by the current regulatory system. Given this transportability of milk, there is no need for high Florida milk production in order to assure an adequate supply for consumption in Florida.

Summary of Effects of Proposed Remedy. The primary beneficial effect that would result from lowering the fluid differential would be to diminish the problem of chronic surpluses of grade A milk. Other desirable effects of narrowing the fluid differential would be:

(1) A reduction in blend price fluctuations;
(2) A reduction in the grade A conversion problem (which is really the oversupply problem in another form).[1]
(3) Increased transportation of milk, but at *lower* delivered cost to the less efficient production regions;
(4) Slightly lower incomes for grade A producers and slightly higher incomes for grade B producers;
(5) Continued "orderly marketing," particularly if reconstitution is permitted (provided the change in the price structure is not too abrupt).[2]

The option of *phased* lowering of the fluid differential would thus lower the social costs of milk regulation, lower the prices paid by fluid milk consumers, lower the total sum paid by consumers for all milk products, lower grade A farmers' incomes (with 50 percent of the decrease accruing to the largest 15 percent of dairy farmers), and raise the incomes of the generally smaller scale grade B milk operations. At the same time, the minimum pricing system would still be

---

[1] See generally, Truman F. Graf and Robert E. Jacobson, *Resolving Grade B Conversion and Low Class I Utilization Pricing and Pooling Problems*, University of Wisconsin-Madison, College of Agricultural and Life Sciences, Research Division, R2503 (June 1973); and J. Robert Strain et al., *The Associated Reserve Standby Pool Cooperative, Past Performance and Future Prospects*, Standby Pool Cooperative Study Committee (March 9, 1973).

[2] The original report included a section on a proposed remedy to eliminate barriers to reconstituted milk.

intact and the blend price mechanism would play the same role as before, except that the federal order blend price would fluctuate *less* after the differential was lowered. Marketing would be protected by minimum prices and would be as orderly as it is currently, but milk would cost less upon receipt by the handler than in the past.

Analysis. Much of the analysis contained in this report has revolved around the classified/blend price structure and the considerations underlying Class I pricing policy. Many of the problems associated with milk marketing today are derived from classified pricing, and the larger the spread in class prices, the greater the problems. Charging a higher price for Class I milk discourages fluid consumption. The higher the Class I differential, the more consumption that is discouraged. The greater the Class I differential, the greater the surplus production. The greater the differential, the more farm prices fluctuate. Price alignment dictates ever-increasing surpluses to the north. These are clearly identifiable problems and undesirable effects of using this form of regulation in achieving an "adequate supply" of milk. If no alternative, efficient means exist to assure an adequate supply of milk, then these problems and effects have to be tolerated if the adequate supply goal is still perceived as a desired one. The problems and effects simply reflect some of the costs that must be borne to reach this goal. However, the proposed remedy of lowering Class I differentials would effectuate the purposes of the act at least as well as the current approach and at lower costs to society.

It was noted earlier that several dairy economists have suggested that a surplus of 20 percent above fluid consumption is sufficient to provide a market with an adequate supply of milk. These statements implicitly or explicitly stand for an adequate supply of milk *from local sources* (that is, from within the same order). The congressional mandate is based on a consumption standard, however, and does not require that the sources be local sources, but only that adequate milk be available. This fact was recognized in the hearing on the issuance of the new Upper Midwest order which certainly has more than adequate supplies for local consumption.[3] Thus, although three, or possibly two, decades ago, maintaining a 20 percent *local* reserve might well have been necessary to satisfy the congressional mandate of assuring supplies adequate for consumption, it is no longer the case. A market may easily satisfy the mandate by importing milk year-round and carrying no surplus. In the month of September 1976, when the Chicago order carried about 225 percent surplus, the new

---

[3] 41 Fed. Reg. 12436 (March 25, 1976).

Upper Midwest order about 180 percent surplus, and the system as a whole about 86 percent surplus, the Florida market was assured of an adequate supply without carrying its 13 percent surplus. (The surplus for the southeastern United States rises to 20 percent when the Georgia and Appalachian order markets are included.)[4] Despite the fact that the goal of adequate supply could be realized without these local surpluses, the fluid differential has been raised in these southern markets to so high a level that they do carry their own surplus.

In fact, one finds that today's federal order system is very well designed to satisfy the goal of assuring an adequate supply of (primarily) *local milk* for fluid consumption, despite the "disruptive" pressures of modern technology. One USDA publication states that the reason why a greater percentage of milk is regulated today than in the 1950s is that, as transport technology became better, producers in unregulated areas had problems keeping "over adequate supplies" of outside milk out of their markets.[5] The system is designed as if the Florida price were set sufficiently high to result in local production, and this was the first price selected. Given this local production philosophy, it then follows that, if the Class I prices in Eau Claire, Chicago, Nashville, or Atlanta are any lower than the Florida price minus freight to Florida (that is, if the other price plus freight to Florida was lower than the Florida price), the whole system would start to collapse. Handlers in other markets could then bottle milk and undercut Florida bottled milk in stores. This would lower the Florida utilization rate, creating an exit of Florida farmers and a dependence upon nonlocal milk. In contrast, if instead the prices in these other cities vastly exceed the Florida price minus freight, then any milk shortage in Florida would have to create a radical price increase before it would be profitable to ship outside milk into the Florida market to satisfy fluid demand. In addition, these higher Class I prices would be in markets like Chicago which already have vast surpluses of milk. A higher fluid differential in these markets would only expand current unneeded surpluses and cost consumers even more.

This analysis explains why there is currently a large surplus in the new Upper Midwest order and in the Chicago order. The way to

---

[4] U.S. Department of Agriculture, Agricultural Marketing Service, *Federal Milk Order Marketing Statistics, September 1976 Summary* (November 1976).

[5] U.S. Department of Agriculture, Consumer and Marketing Service, *The Federal Milk Marketing Order Program*, Marketing Bulletin 27 (April 1968), p. 11. See also Alden C. Manchester, *Pricing Milk and Dairy Products: Principles, Practices, and Problems*, U.S. Department of Agriculture, Economic Research Service, Agricultural Economic Report No. 207 (June 1971), p. 7, n. 2.

lower the Chicago surplus is to lower the Chicago Class I price, but to do so would undercut the whole system. Chicago milk delivered to other markets would become cheaper than the indigenous milk in those markets.[6] Once an Upper Midwest price is established based on the goal of local production in Florida, the system will function with the least fluctuations if other areas are then charged prices based on the Upper Midwest price, plus freight, regardless of destination.

Consider the alternative of lowering the fluid differentials in all of the federal orders by 10 cents. This would lower the price of a gallon of milk by approximately 1 cent. The effect on the blend price received by farmers would be much less than 10 cents. For any Class II price, the decline in the blend price is found as approximately the utilization rate times the change in the Class I price. If the Class I utilization were 60 percent, the blend price would fall by 6 cents. If the blend price were to fall by 6 cents per hundredweight from a previous price of about $10, statistical studies on dairy industry supply response indicate that dairy output would fall by less than 1 percent and probably only about 0.5 percent.[7] A drop in supply of 0.5 percent would translate into approximately a 1 percent drop in the output of manufactured milk products and an *increase* in the Class II price. This partially offsets the 6-cents downward effect on the blend price because of the lower Class I price, thus attenuating the supply effect. The supply effect would thus be a reduction equal to less than 0.5 percent of the milk. The effect on farm supply of local milk in Florida could conceivably be slightly more than 0.5 percent. Even if it were, Florida would still have an adequate supply of local milk for fluid consumption, and vast surpluses of easily transported milk would still be available in many markets capable of shipping milk to Florida. Without changing the basic existing system, *the fluid differential could conceivably be narrowed by 70 cents to $1 without jeopardizing an adequate supply of milk to Florida.* This requires that adequate supply be tested under standards involving demand and stable prices, not production.

Adjunct changes that would facilitate an adequate supply of milk to market areas during short periods might include a liberalization of

[6] Because of today's high transport costs, the Chicago and Upper Midwest Class I prices could be cut substantially, helping consumers in these areas and in the South, without undercutting the whole system, and with a relatively small impact on farmer blend prices.

[7] For example, D. Chen, R. Courtney, and A. Schmitz, "A Polynomial Lag Formulation of Milk Production Response," *American Journal of Agricultural Economics*, vol. 54 (February 1972), pp. 77–83; and H. W. Halvorson, "The Response of Milk Production to Price," *Journal of Farm Economics*, vol. 40 (August 1958), pp. 1101–13.

the allocation provisions to encourage interorder shipments in time of relative shortage, and modification of base-plan provisions.

Markets with base plans tend to retain, and even attract, milk during the fall months. A producer (or cooperative) in a base-plan market will suffer a loss if he sends milk to a short market in the fall because, if that market does not take his milk during the spring, he can only earn the excess price in his own market during the spring. Florida, for instance, is virtually surrounded by markets with base plans. Methods could be developed to compensate for this base-plan problem if it was concluded that base plans should be retained, although their usefulness may disappear when the surpluses are reduced.

If these administrative changes were instituted, how would the operation of milk markets be affected? Farmers would convert to grade A production only if the average annual blend price exceeded the additional costs of conversion. Assume that the grade A price must exceed the grade B price by 15 cents per hundredweight for this conversion to occur.[8] To abstract, assume a market with some grade B production and an annual supply cycle in which spring utilization was equal to 80 percent and winter and summer utilization was equal to 90 percent of fall utilization. If each season were three months long, the fluid differential necessary to have 100 percent of bottling needs *in the fall* would be 16.66 cents per hundredweight during that period. The blend price would fall to 13.3 cents above the Class II price in the spring. If the cycle were to vary from 50 percent in the spring to only 90 percent in the fall and 70 percent in between, the fluid differential would have to be 21.5 cents and the blend price would fluctuate 8.6 cents between 10.7 cents and 19.3 cents above the Class II price, averaging annually 15 cents above the Class II price. The small size of these price fluctuations (as compared to what is currently observed) is because of the smaller fluid differential. (To put these figures in context, given the same utilization figures and a fluid differential of $2.15, the blend would fluctuate 86 cents between $1.07 and $1.93 above the Class II price.)

If such a scheme were designed to have only enough grade A milk in the fall to satisfy the entire United States, the fluid differentials and blend price fluctuations in the long run would, as today, be greater as one moved south from the primary, grade B production area in the Upper Midwest. However, the fluid differentials and blend price fluctuations would be narrower than those observed today. (The geographic area of grade B production would be wider as well.) If

---

[8] Graf and Jacobson, *Resolving Grade B Conversion and Low Class I Utilization Pricing and Pooling Problems*, p. 60.

differentials were to be lowered to this level today, blend prices would be even closer to the Class II price initially because there is currently more grade A milk than needed during the fall. Reverting to grade B from grade A saves less per hundredweight than the costs of moving from grade B to grade A, so it would take some time for the long-run solution to result.

Other results expected to flow from narrowing the differentials are that utilization rates would continue to vary less (in percentage terms) in markets progressively farther from the Upper Midwest; that seasonal production and transportation cycles would be wider; that pooling and transportation cycles would be wider; and that pooling requirements would have to specify more fall shipments from Class II plants in order to maintain orderly marketing channels. In practice, one would expect moderate Class I premiums to become common in the fall; a reduction in the Class II price to below the M-W price (perhaps 15 cents or 20 cents); a Class I differential slightly greater than in the theoretical construct; and a desire to have enough grade A milk in the fall to satisfy unusually short milk production (or high-demand) years. But, by raising supply-plant pooling requirements, a much narrower fluid differential could assure an adequate supply of milk for fluid purposes in a more nationally oriented market scheme.

The difficulties associated with implementing this possible remedy create separate problems. The problems encountered are, however, common to other reforms, and are addressed separately below.

Phased Deregulation of Milk Marketing

Another possible remedy we wish to examine in depth is that of deregulation of the federal order system, through a phasing out of the classified pricing mechanism. This phased removal does not imply that milk will not be sold on the basis of (verified) weights and tests; nor should it be interpreted as a policy which would reduce the cooperative marketing of milk. Rather, deregulation would probably increase the cooperative marketing of milk in the United States.

Summary of Effects of Proposed Remedy. Because an unregulated system would be vastly different from the current system of milk marketing, it is difficult to summarize the process by which the many effects of deregulation would go about solving the problems discussed in the report. The most significant of these processes will be discussed at more length in the analysis. However, it is accurate to generalize that one would expect orderly marketing relationships to develop if a gradual deregulation of the federal order system were instituted.

Analysis. Because the unregulated system is a highly complex system of marketing, the analysis is divided into three sections. We shall first look at what deregulation would imply if the market for milk were "static," that is, if equilibrium were restored instantly. This is useful for identifying the direction in which the market will respond. Next, the fact that there are annual cycles in milk production and in milk demand will be considered. Finally, we shall examine what a deregulated system would look like when there are also possibilities of "random shocks," that is, external events of an unexpected nature that affect the supply and demand for milk.[9] The analysis of how the deregulated market would operate is undertaken at this time *without* consideration of transition problems or of equity considerations. These matters are addressed below.

The federal order system of classified pricing was developed in the 1930s through a series of "emergency legislations" based on the marketing conditions being faced by the dairy industry at the time. In the 1920s farmer bargaining was expressly sanctioned for the first time in the United States. Farmer cooperatives started to develop means of offsetting the monopsonistic power of purchasers of raw milk. This monopsonistic power arose because raw milk was extremely perishable, on-farm refrigeration was virtually nonexistent, and transport technology was extremely crude. A farmer, or a small cooperative of farmers, in the absence of their traditional market outlet would find it extremely expensive to find alternative outlets for their milk. In today's markets milk can easily be shipped great distances to markets which can be located readily by cooperative personnel and/or milk brokers. If a particular processor reduces its needs for raw milk, then the farmer is no longer faced with the alternative of spoiled product, but rather the alternative of shipping product to another processor. The 1930s were also the period of the Depression, and milk prices were declining rapidly. One of the considerations of the Congress was to keep farmers' prices up to keep them from "over-disinvesting" in milk production. The fear was that the *temporary* decline in milk prices would lead to too many farmers going out of business so that, when the general economy reestablished itself, milk prices would be very high for a substantial period of time.

---

[9] See Manchester, *Pricing Milk and Dairy Products*, pp. 3–4: "Static concepts of price theory provide a basis for understanding the pricemaking process, but full recognition of the essential dynamic character of this process is necessary for complete understanding of its operation."

More than just a year or two would pass before more people would reenter dairy farming. This justification for maintaining milk regulation is, of course, no longer pertinent.

Regardless of one's definition for the phrase "orderly marketing," one would not have called many of the markets where federal regulation was first imposed orderly. Even after the advent of federal (and state) regulation of milk marketing, however, much of the milk in the United States was sold in *unregulated* markets. As of 1945, eight years after the passage of the Agricultural Marketing Agreements Act, about 40 percent of the fluid grade milk sold in the United States was not subject to either federal or state regulation of producer prices. As late as 1955, about 25 percent of fluid grade milk was not under federal or state regulation.[10]

Even during those time periods when milk was still relatively difficult to transport great distances and refrigeration technology was not as highly developed as it is today, a high proportion of the fluid markets were not state regulated and had not opted for federal regulation. There are at least two basic incentives to ask for federal regulation. One incentive exists if there are the unstable marketing relationships often referred to under the rubric of "disorderly marketing." The other incentive is to obtain higher prices for milk. During the time that costs of converting grade B production to grade A production declined, federal regulations have not decreased the fluid differentials (the difference between the Class I and Class II price), but have increased them. Therefore, the *price* incentive for voting in a federal order has increased during this time. More than 95 percent of the grade A milk in the United States is now subject to federal or state regulation.[11] Thus, as the factors which would lead to "disorderly marketing" have declined or virtually disappeared, the proportion of milk under regulation has increased radically,[12] at a time when one would have anticipated less regulation, except for the incentive for higher prices.

The static unregulated market. How would an unregulated market function if it existed in today's economy? If the markets for milk

---

[10] Alden C. Manchester, *Market Structure, Institutions, and Performance in the Fluid Milk Industry*, U.S. Department of Agriculture, Economic Research Service, Agricultural Economic Report No. 248 (1974). In the last decade, both the Chicago and the Mississippi orders were suspended for long periods pursuant to requests by the dominant cooperatives in these markets.

[11] Ibid.

[12] Additionally, some disorderly marketing was a result of a function of selling milk without verified weights and tests—a problem which would not result today as a necessary consequence of deregulation. With bulk tanks and cooperative testing facilities, these types of problems are vastly reduced.

were static, a deregulated and competitive system for milk sales would lead to grade A milk being sold at a particular place with a particular delivery schedule and set of services being priced at a single price, regardless of the final utilization of that milk. Deregulation would lead to a drop in the price of milk being sold for fluid bottling toward the price of milk being used for manufacturing. As this process occurred, dairy farmers' incomes would fall and the quantity of fluid milk consumed would increase. The combination of these factors would lead to a slightly lower total supply of grade A milk, with more grade A milk being used for fluid bottling and, consequently, less milk going into manufactured products. The price for milk used in manufacturing would be higher than under regulation.

One computer simulation for the effects of deregulation developed a series of "conservative estimates" based on the assumptions that southern markets would have to import at least some milk from northern markets (retaining price alignment) and that the sale of reconstituted milk would continue to be prohibited. The simulation estimated that the price of milk for manufacturing uses (both grade A and grade B) would increase on the order of 38 cents per hundredweight (about 4 cents a pound for cheese and ice cream and 8 cents a pound for butter) with deregulation, and the price of milk for fluid uses would decline on the order of 63 cents per hundredweight (5.5 cents a gallon). With both influences occurring at the same time, the estimates indicate a decrease in the farm price for grade A milk on the order of 25 cents per hundredweight (approximately 3 percent) and an increase in the price of grade B milk of approximately 38 cents (approximately 5 percent). These estimates are conservative, but they indicate, under these assumptions, a decrease in grade A milk production in the United States of approximately 2 percent and a decrease in total (grade A and grade B) milk production of approximately 1.3 percent. They also indicate a decrease in consumer expenditures on the order of $200 million a year. Decreases in milk production of this order of magnitude are small even when compared to the average yearly amount of milk which is "removed" from the system by support price purchases in the United States.[13]

However, allowing for two other factors makes the impact somewhat larger. There will be three distinct types of markets under deregulation. These markets can be characterized as surplus, import, and intermediate. A surplus market is one that has enough milk

---

[13] See U.S. Department of Agriculture, Economic Research Service, *Dairy Situation* (May 1976). In almost all years, "removals" exceed 2 percent of supply and they have reached 10 percent of supply.

throughout the year to engage in manufacturing. An import market is one that must meet its fluid needs by importing at least some grade A milk at all times of the year. The intermediate market is one that can fulfill fluid needs in the spring with local production but must import milk in the fall. The previously described projections were conservative by comparison because midwestern markets were treated as surplus markets (as they should be) and all other markets were treated as import markets. (The exclusion of intermediate markets, as defined, is one factor that makes the above estimates conservative.)

In any southern market where total milk production exceeds fluid needs to the extent that some milk goes into manufactured dairy products year-round, the price of manufacturing milk could not rise above the price of manufacturing milk in the more efficient northern markets. In such markets the decrease in the price of fluid milk to consumers would be greater and the farm price would drop more radically as well. The supply by farmers in such markets would also decrease more than under the conservative estimates. The decrease in supply in those markets will *not* be so great as to create a shortage of milk for fluid bottling in those markets. To argue that those markets would be short of milk for fluid bottling would be to argue that the markets are not isolated and are indeed dependent upon some amount of milk imports from markets with milk, contrary to the initial stipulation. Because milk can now move great distances, there is an effective maximum on the local price of milk for fluid bottling equal to the cost of importing milk to the market for that purpose. When such a price is achieved, the fluid needs of the market will be maintained by imported milk, and the local farm price in such a market will be an "all fluid" price.

If the farm price in the market is an "all fluid" price, then it equals a price which is a fluid price in a distant market plus transport cost to the southern market. But if farm prices were that high in the southern market, we would then return to the situation of higher farm prices. This would represent less of a supply restriction than would have been implied by the concept of the fluid price falling to the manufacturing price in the Upper Midwest. In other words, the prices to consumers must fall at least as much as the prices to consumers in alternative markets (such as the Upper Midwest) plus import costs of milk. With the Upper Midwest price falling, it follows that the consumer prices must fall in each market, whether or not that market experiences large declines in milk production. Also, because of the long-distance transport capabilities of milk, it follows that the fluid bottling markets within each area will not be short of raw milk for bottling, even though some of the milk might be imported (as is often the case currently). Such imports would be priced significantly lower than the current regulated fluid prices in these markets.

Finally, there is the intermediate type of market, which is not particularly important in the consideration of the static effects of deregulation, but is important in the consideration of the dynamic effects. In this type of market, the fluid price in the spring would not fall to the manufacturing price because the amount of milk in the market would not be so great as to yield any significant milk manufacturing (outside of harder-to-transport manufactured items such as yogurt and ice cream). Instead, in the spring there would be no excess of grade A milk (or excesses would be shipped to year-round import markets).

Thus, in a static framework, the consumer would realize a cost savings of at least $200 million from deregulation and milk producers would end up with approximately 3 percent lower prices by the most conservative estimates. The consumer cost savings could be substantially larger in cases where farm prices fall farther than predicted generally. There would exist no shortages of milk for fluid bottling in the unregulated system. In some markets, however, demand for fluid bottling might be satisfied with greater milk imports from other areas than is currently the case. The amount imported from other areas would rise during the fall and decline in the spring. Milk brokerage and/or advantages of cooperative regionalization would increase under such a situation. Generally, one would expect a "dominoing" of milk supplies (area A ships to area B, B ships to C, and so forth) to become more prevalent than it is currently.

The dynamic unregulated market. The next factor to be injected into the analysis is the annual cycle of milk production and demand. As a first order of magnitude approximation of what would occur, we shall consider the demand and supply cycles as if they were absolutely predictable. (The possibility of "random shocks" is considered below.) There are two basic problems in this area, and they are important because the production/demand cycles and the existence of the two grades of milk are factors that have *not* changed over the years. The first is the problem of grade B versus grade A milk production. The second is the question of the spatial character of markets—in particular, in the intermediate group of markets which have insufficient local supplies for fluid needs in the fall, but surpluses in the spring.

The first basic principle of importance is that a *predictable* price cycle is no burden to the dairy farmer because the dairy farmer, like other farmers, makes long-term production decisions. Currently, dairy farm prices and dairy farmers' incomes vary over an annual cycle in the federal order system. Because of the blend price mechanism, farmers' prices vary over the cycles *more* than consumer prices in all markets.

After deregulation, the magnitude of the annual cycle in some markets could be greater than the current one; in other markets, it might be substantially less. Consumer prices would vary with farm prices under deregulation. This creates no problem as long as the annual spectrum of returns is basically known. For instance, farmers who produce a single annual crop are only earning in that crop during a few months out of the year. This does not mean that they decide not to grow the crop, only that they must plan their annual consumption around their annual income.

It is also true that permitting price fluctuations in line with supply fluctuations over such a predictable cycle is to the consumer's benefit. To smooth out consumer prices and have a supply adequate to meet demand at those smooth prices even during the low supply period requires that the average price paid by consumers over the year be higher than the average price the consumer would pay if the prices were permitted to fluctuate. If, instead, consumer prices were set at a nonfluctuating level equal to the *average price* they would pay over the course of a year if prices were allowed to fluctuate as in an unregulated market, farmers would target about the same annual production level. Thus, the supply of milk during the short production period would be inadequate to satisfy consumer demands at that price.[14] Thus, the artificial smoothing of consumer prices will make the average price higher. In the case where there are predictable price cycles, allowing the prices to fluctuate with the supply cycle is not to the disadvantage of the farmer and it is to the advantage of the consumer. With those considerations in mind, we can turn to examining the grade B–grade A conversion problem in a market without regulation.

The grade B–grade A problem is simply the effect on cyclical price fluctuations because of the existence of two grades of milk. Grade A milk can be substituted for grade B; the reverse is not true. Short of the socially expensive option of mandating a single grade of milk, in an unregulated market with only predictable price cycles, the grade B–grade A problem could lead to wider price fluctuations than

---

[14] With deregulation, but a predictable milk cycle, virtually all (that is, more than 90 percent) grade A milk would be in fluid use during the fall. If consumers were to pay only the average deregulated price year-round, their demand would be greater in the fall. To satisfy this demand would require more fall milk production. To get more grade A milk production would require an even higher annual average grade A price. The higher price must come from consumers.

would occur in a regulated market with narrowed fluid differentials. These cycles could be radically reduced by the influences of reconstituted or partially reconstituted product. However, we examine this possibility only after some consideration of the harder case without reconstitution.

First, consider a northern market with both grade B and grade A milk production. During the spring the grade A price for fluid milk would fall to the grade B price. Fall revenues would have to be sufficient to make the average annual price at least 15 cents in excess of the grade B price.[15] If the short season were only two months a year, the Class I price would have to rise relative to the grade B price to a level of 90 cents per hundredweight (8 cents a gallon) for those months to encourage grade A production. However, handlers and producers might find it profitable to have a smaller price cycle. If a handler had enough regular milk for the fall, but needed the milk of 25 percent more cows during the fall, the handler, or one of its supplying cooperatives, could get a standby reserve by a payment of 15 cents per hundredweight on a year-round basis to producers who would otherwise be in grade B production. The cost of this reserve supply would be less than 4 cents per hundredweight on the plants' total supply. In a deregulated market (without any cooperative holding a very large market share) such a standby pool option (much like the Associated Reserve Standby Pool Cooperative) would be a competitive response rather than a monopolistic device.

The spatial area of a market's milk supply would vary over the annual cycle in an unregulated market. Again, we recognize that a reconstituted (or partially reconstituted) product would reduce the significance of spatial influences. However, our preliminary description considers the geographic parameters of markets without reconstituted product being available.

The three types of markets already referred to (that is, surplus, import, and intermediate) would have three distinct behavior patterns. Markets that relied on some imported milk year-round would be, in percentage terms, the most stable markets. The prices in these markets would approximate surplus area production prices plus transport over the annual cycle. Thus, the price in these markets would fluctuate with prices in the surplus markets. Processors or cooperatives in import markets could have options to purchase milk during the short season with processors or cooperatives in these surplus areas. The surplus areas would thus be compensated for carrying the re-

---

[15] Because of fluctuations in capacity utilization, the manufacturing price of grade A milk in some markets could fall somewhat short of the grade B price for a substantial part of the year.

serves of the shorter production areas, shipping much more milk in the fall than during the balance of the year. The advantages of phased deregulation over rapid deregulation should be clear, as time would be required to develop commercial relationships for handling a perishable product in the most orderly fashion.

The markets with the least price stability would be in the intermediate markets, those that rely on imported milk during the fall but have surplus milk during the spring. In the spring the price would fall to a manufacturing level. Again, if there were no unpredictable demand and/or supply shifts, except for changes in the average annual price level, these price cycles are not to the disadvantage of producers. Additionally, allowing a cycle permits a lower annual average price, to the advantage of consumers. The effects of demand and/or supply uncertainty will be considered below.

The above analysis proceeds on the assumption that reconstituted product is not available. However, the process by which reconstituted product would dampen the price cycles should now be explained.

The price of milk used in manufacturing would exhibit only a narrow price cycle over the year because of the storability of milk powder, cheese, and some other manufactured products. The prices of milk powder and cheese would be even more stable over the annual cycles. For ease of explanation we assume that milk powder keeps the same price over the annual cycle. Therefore, the price of reconstituted product would also remain stable throughout the annual cycle. If the fluid price rose by 20 cents a gallon, then it would have risen by 20 cents relative to the price of reconstituted product and 10 cents a gallon relative to the price of milk which is only 50 percent reconstituted product. In a market where raw milk is imported only part of the year, the reconstituted product would be at least as expensive as whole milk during the spring. As the price of raw milk started to rise, reconstituted product would thus become relatively cheaper.[16] If, as the differential between raw and reconstituted product widened, this led to 10 percent of fluid sales being composed of fully reconstituted product and 10 percent being composed of a 50 percent mixture of fresh fluid milk and reconstituted product, then 15 percent of total fluid-use milk would be in reconstituted product. Then, even a 15 percent fresh fluid supply deficit relative to demand at the going

---

[16] Some observers have asserted that reconstitution would not be profitable in a deregulated market. If predictable price cycles were very wide, however, it would be profitable to reconstitute in the fall months. If the cited North Carolina price differences are a guide to today's reconstitution technology, then reconstituted milk probably would be sold in several markets for at least part of the year.

price would not lead to a price high enough to attract imports of raw milk from other domestic sources. The market's raw milk price would thus exhibit a much smaller cycle because of milk reconstitution. This would also reduce the cyclical variation in milk transport and the cyclical variation in the use of reserve optioned milk. The impact of the grade B–grade A cyclical problem is correspondingly reduced.

Random shocks in an unregulated market. If something called "disorderly marketing" has an economic cost, it must be because of unpredicted market changes; otherwise, predictable and stable relationships will evolve. Thus, we must analyze how an unregulated market would respond to unpredictable shifts in supply or demand. Although the likelihood of drastic changes is small judging from past experiences, the possibility should be examined. The regulatory system, as currently constituted, has features that make it able to absorb the destabilizing effects of sudden demand booms or supply drops. It also has features that inherently lead to less stability.

The federal order system generates grade A milk production far in excess of fluid needs. This, of course, could act as a buffer in times of sudden short supply relative to demand at the current regulated prices. But the system also destabilizes and creates false grade A shortages in local markets, even though the national surplus is huge.

If the regulatory system, as it is currently conceived, is to be effective, it must somehow reduce excess milk movement when it is not really needed. The natural (and probably necessary) methods of achieving this include supply-plant pooling provisions, diversion provisions, and allocation provisions. Although supply-plant pooling provisions require milk shipments during the fall, in almost all cases (except the new Upper Midwest order) shipment requirements are based on rules that are not self-adjusting on an interannual basis. Short supply conditions south of Chicago lead to southern handlers facing Chicago supply plants whose producers draw the blend price by only shipping 20 percent of their milk to fluid users. A Chicago supply plant would generally find a severe cost disadvantage to pool on another order with (logically required) higher shipping requirements. Both the Chicago plants and the plants in the deficit order would have to be compensated for their lost manufacturing margin to induce them to ship milk. Furthermore, the producers delivering to these plants might be hesitant to sever shipping relationships with the plants in order to ship directly to Class I handlers. They would have little to gain in doing so; they would draw the blend price anyway. Finally, if the handlers in another order did contract to pay enough to get a Chicago plant to ship more than 20 percent of its grade A milk to fluid uses, the importing handler would have to pay the additional costs incurred under the allocation provisions. Although the costs of the allocation provisions fall as shortages appear, such costs generally remain substantial. Milk shortage premiums can develop during the fall and winter months, and grade A milk shortages can develop in markets at the regulated prices. These shortages are true shortages only within the current system of regulation. They are in fact functionally artificial because the milk is there, but supply-plant provisions reduce the incentive to send more than the fixed requirement of milk to Class I uses, and the allocation provisions reduce cross-market milk flows between handlers. A clear indication of this effect is the fact that *processed* product was generally shipped more than raw milk despite the higher costs of moving processed product and, to a lesser extent, the inertia associated with brand name acceptance.[17]

The primary point to keep in mind is that recent milk shortage experiences are caused by individual agents being unable to find enough milk at regulated prices. Such "shortages" occur because the USDA follows a set of pooling rules (reasonable, given regulatory costs) which are consistent with long-run average shipping needs and the attempt to assure an adequate supply of milk for the market *from local sources*. Their policies reduce inefficient milk movement during heavy production periods, and they assure long-run local supplies by inhibiting interorder movements.

In a deregulated system, the least expensive (consistent with scheduling and quality) milk would serve market demands. The artificial shortages created by the pool plant and allocation provisions would be reduced. However, other influences would potentially lead to less interannual stability. These factors are examined here; revisions in support price programs consistent with this analysis are suggested below.

The factors that are important in analyzing unpredictable influences on price cycles are the same as those that are important in analyzing predictable cycles. Markets with more than sufficient grade A milk for fluid use on a year-round basis will be basically unaffected by variations in interannual supply or demand. Without fully predictable price cycles, markets which might experience deficits but regularly have grade B production would have handlers find their individually optimal amount of option contracts to be at slightly higher levels. Option contracts are standby pool payments to potentially grade B producers in order to encourage them to maintain grade

---

[17] See H. L. Forest, Dairy Division, Agricultural Marketing Service, U.S. Department of Agriculture, memorandum entitled "Movements of Milk In and Out of Federal Milk Order Markets," August 8, 1975.

A production. Such option payments would vastly reduce the cycles, and would do so more effectively than did ARSPC.

ARSPC milk was subject to allocation provisions and compensatory payments. Even though these payments were absorbed by ARSPC, their costs are imbedded in the stated ARSPC price and annual option cost, making actual shipments artificially expensive. In addition, since ARSPC was developed to keep milk from moving competitively, the option payment was higher than that of similar options purchased competitively, because ARSPC made it prohibitively expensive for nonmembers to get milk options for bona fide standby reserve milk. This left reserve milk selectively available at best.

If the aggregate of the individual decision units "under-optioned" milk, and fluid demand went beyond grade A production, including grade A milk shipments, then the raw milk price would start to exhibit a marked increase in all three types of markets. Again, a price increase because of a bona fide shortage, if such a degree of shortage did ever occur, would be dampened by the stocks of powdered milk and the ability to sell reconstituted (or partially reconstituted) product. The grade A shortage would have to be much more massive than experience dictates before the result would be a substantial shortage-induced price rise. Thus, any price cycles in surplus markets or in markets that would be dependent on milk from such areas on a year-round basis would experience very little interannual price uncertainty. Because the price cycle would be smaller in such markets after deregulation with a continuation of price supports similar to those used today, these markets might well experience less interannual price uncertainty than with the federal order system. A changed price support system could reduce this uncertainty even further.

The intermediate type of market (some should exist even with the use of reconstituted product) would face considerable interannual variation based on the cycle within a single year. Although the fall import price and the spring surplus season prices would be as predictable as in other markets, they may be far apart. As explained above, there is no economic harm in a predictable price cycle, even if it is large. Although the high and low prices in the cycle would be relatively predictable, the portion of the year over which the higher price is received could vary widely between years, creating substantial interannual risk.

It should first be pointed out that this cycle is not a great disadvantage to consumers, even if some farmers exit from dairy farming who would have remained in production for the same average expected rate of return without this random variation. Sometimes it has been stated that this uncertainty would lead to (all) farmers exiting the market, leading to outrageously high consumer prices. This is a variant of the "lower price leads to lessened production and consequently higher prices" fallacy.

In the intermediate type of market, if 20 percent of the producers went out of production because of the posited interannual instability of the intra-annual price cycle, the posited instability would disappear. The market would have raw milk prices dictated by the relatively stable import price year-round. This price would be lower than the current price because of the deregulation, and consumers would benefit. As exit of farmers who feared risk occurred, the risk would be reduced. The exit because of the degree of risk would cease no later than the time when the small number of exiting farmers necessary to make the market continually an import market had occurred and probably well before that point.

In conclusion then, we would expect orderly marketing relationships to develop if a gradual deregulation of the federal order system were instituted.

Price/Income Support Reform

Some of the possible remedies discussed above will likely be criticized because they will be viewed as changing the general price levels for dairy products, leading to uncertainty and premature exit of farmers from dairying.

The problem of general price level changes can be vastly ameliorated by the dissemination of information by the USDA. (This is already done, for essentially the same reason, for many crops.) Overreaction to changing price levels is unlikely, but any remaining problematic tendency may be virtually eliminated by phasing in the possible remedies rather than effecting abrupt changes which may lead to abrupt reactions.

Despite the fact that fear of overreaction on the part of dairy farmers is probably misplaced, programs can be instituted that are specifically designed to handle the problem of premature exit. The most promising types of plans for allowing the farmer to avoid the risks of insolvency on a cash flow basis are either a variable price support program or a form of milk price insurance.[18]

A price support program could easily be devised that supports milk prices at 95 percent of some measure of the margin of average price over direct production costs for the previous five years of production. Although "parity" as a concept is economically invalid and

---

[18] Federally insured loan programs would be of some help as well.

inefficient over long time periods (that is, if the base years are a decade or more earlier), it is more useful over a short term. For example, the government could guarantee support purchases if prices fall below 95 percent of the (weighted) average parity level of the previous five years. Further dampening can be achieved by beginning to purchase when price levels fall to 97 percent of this average. This would also stabilize future prices in manufactured milk products. Such a program, if intended to reduce variability—the primary element of risk—might also dictate sales of government stocks to limit price increases beyond 105 percent of the average. One-sided programs may be justified, however, providing the 95 percent average is based on previous price/direct production cost margins (adjusting any large margin to 105 percent of its previous year's margin). An advantage of the systematic two-sided program is that government support purchases may be released back to the market rather than merely operating as a one-way street.[19] Some form of this moving average price support, particularly with partial support when prices first start to drop, might well prove to be a better stabilizer of the market than the current program.

Beyond this type of national support system, price risk could be virtually removed by a system of voluntary price insurance. The notion behind this insurance would be to give any farmer the ability to make his income as stable as the national price support will make the average national price. A farmer could decide to take the insurance on any portion of his production, measured in units,[20] from zero to 100 percent. The percentage that his price is of the national average price is calculated for each of the previous five years. To the extent his price falls below its historical average of the past five years by more than 5 percent, he is reimbursed by the system for any deficit incurred for the amount of his output covered. To the extent his price rises more than 5 percent above the average, he pays in the surplus for the same amount of output covered. The farmer would at any time be able to get this insurance, to commence one year after electing coverage. The output covered could be changed to any desired amount (possibly with a maximum annual change), not to exceed current output, to start one year after the changed amount is specified.

---

[19] By our definition of a support program we are referring to true supports. Programs like the school milk program should be based on the government's purchasing the desired supplies regardless of the farmer's price.

[20] If it were measured in percentages, a high insurance coverage would have the undesirable effect of encouraging a farmer to expand supply during high supply-low price years and contract during low supply-high price years.

Summary of Effects of Proposed Remedy. The variable price support program would reduce the risks of insolvency on a cash flow basis that dairy farmers face.

However, it is both an advantage and a disadvantage of a price support program that it slows production response to demand and supply changes. If the changes are short-term random shocks and if overreaction is considered a possibility, this is an advantage. But, if the changes reflect long-term shifts in supply or demand, a price support program is a disadvantage. The (weighted) average approach assures reasonably rapid reflection of long-term changes with a recognition of the likelihood of short-term shocks.

The insurance program would provide an additional means of a dairy farmer protecting himself from unexpected market changes. That program would allow any desired amount of voluntary income smoothing, would be structured to allow for inflation, would maintain full local supply response to changes in local supply and demand conditions, and, by building in the one-year anticipation period, would avoid farmers' applying only after local supply conditions make a rapid shift.

Under these conditions, consumers would benefit from the advantages that flow from letting prices adjust to supply and demand conditions and farmers would be able to choose voluntarily any amount of income smoothing. This would reduce the possibility of farmers' reacting with socially incorrect production responses.

Analysis. Having described some reform possibilities and how those reforms would affect the congressionally declared policy of assuring adequate supplies of milk for fluid consumption, the remaining issue is what effect the reforms would have on the net income of dairy farmers in general. Congress expressed concern over the level of net income to dairy farmers, and the issue of dairy farm income is invariably raised in connection with reform of the regulation of milk marketing. The view is widely held that the incomes of milk producers should be protected. (Implicit in the current system, but never stated, is that this has come to mean protecting grade A producers at the expense of grade B producers.)

There are two basic questions. The first is whether we should, as a matter of equity and public policy, subsidize dairy farmers; the second is whether such a policy has desirable effects on the economic system in general.

The first question can ultimately be answered only by the political process. Special interest legislation is commonplace, and a not-inappropriate characteristic of a democratic system. If subsidized dairy farming is seen as a desirable end in itself, then there is little to be gained by questioning that decision. If, however, protecting producer income is claimed to offer benefits to society, and is only a means to an end, then analysis of the effects is a desirable aid to the political process. In addition, the efficiency of the method by which incomes are protected or enhanced is a proper issue, regardless of the motivation behind the program.

Conclusions that have been reached in previous sections of the report regarding the impact of milk regulation on producer income include the following: First, the federal order system subsidizes grade A farmers (that is, farmer-owners) at a large cost to society. This cost would be reduced (or almost eradicated) by the introduction of direct payments to these farmers in the form of a lump-sum tax write-off or by a direct payment. This could raise dairy farmers' incomes while increasing consumer value.

Second, the current system subsidizes larger (generally more affluent) grade A farmer-owners to a proportionally greater extent than it does smaller farmers. Larger dairy farms, comprising only 3.3 percent of total farms, receive 23.8 percent of the subsidies.[21] A lump-sum tax write-off or welfare payment would lead to more income equality and would help the family farm without giving an even greater subsidy to the large farms.

Third, lower income grade B farmers are financially hurt by the system. Under plausible assumptions, their income is lowered by an amount equal to about $100 million, whereas grade A producers are only benefited by about $180 million.[22]

Fourth, farmer *income* in the United States is now almost at parity with nonfarm incomes, a radical change from earlier decades when the current programs were being developed.[23]

Fifth, the primary beneficiaries of these programs are *landowners*

---

[21] It has been estimated that 15.5 percent of the farms receive 6 percent of the subsidy income. Calculated from data contained in: U.S. Department of Agriculture, Economic Research Service, *The Impact of Dairy Imports on the U.S. Dairy Industry*, a Report for the U.S. Congress, Senate, Committee on Agriculture and Forestry, 93rd Congress, 2d session, January 2, 1975.

[22] Richard Ippolito and Robert T. Masson, "The Social Cost of Government Regulation of Milk" (unpublished paper, October 1976).

[23] For 1972, 1973, and 1974, per capita disposable farm income from all sources was 81 percent, 107 percent, and 92 percent of per capita nonfarm income, respectively. Both sets of figures include return on capital (for example, the incomes of owners of large farms and earnings on invested capital of industrialists are included). The farm income also includes the income of resident farm laborers. The figures contrast sharply with even the period 1959–1961 when per capita farm incomes as a percentage of nonfarm income were 48 percent, 53 percent, and 57 percent, respectively. U.S. Department of Agriculture, *Agricultural Statistics 1975* (1975), p. 464.

in grade A production areas. Over one-fourth of the dairy acreage is not operated by owners. These nonowner farmers and farm laborers receive little of the subsidy. Those who owned farms when regulation was implemented received their subsidy first in higher income, and second by selling their land at higher prices because of its higher value in production. Subsequent land purchasers paid for this subsidy in inflated land values and have been lesser beneficiaries of the system. If the subsidy amounts to $200 million a year and there are approximately 300,000 dairy farmers who can borrow money at roughly 10 percent interest, the annual subsidy is about $666.67 per farmer, and the inflation in land value is about $6,666.67 per farm. For the top 3.3 percent of grade A owner-farmers this is $5,000 a year or $50,000 per farm. For the smallest 45 percent, the subsidy amounts to $100 a year or $1,000 per farm.[24]

The answer to the second question, whether the federal order subsidy has desirable *economic effects* to society, is more clear. There is no *net* economic advantage in raising dairy farmers' incomes except possibly for raising incomes during a minority of years in which prices and/or incomes are unusually suppressed. A commonly heard contention about any program which may lower farmers' incomes goes as follows:

> If you institute this program, farmers' prices and incomes will fall. Because of their lower incomes they will go out of business. Then consumers will have to pay much more for milk because there will be so little of it.

This statement clearly refers to dynamic overadjustments as a reduction in demand does not yield a higher price in any case.

In a dynamic context, it is true that lower prices may lead to excess exit of producers and thus higher prices. The timing sequence and the assumptions about farmer behavior are crucial to this explanation. The fundamental assumption is that farmers will overreact to a price change. First, as (effective) demand declines, farmers must all see the ensuing price change as large and they must assume that the price will remain consistently and substantially below the previous price. This means that each farmer assumes that other farmers will not overreact by reducing production significantly and that few will go out of business despite the fact that it is clear to each individual farmer that prices are unremunerative and it is in fact time to go out of business. If farmers myopically overreact by exiting from the market before they realize others are exiting as well, and if they overreact

[24] Calculated from the tables in U.S. Department of Agriculture, *The Impact of Dairy Imports on the U.S. Dairy Industry.*

before exit starts to reestablish prices, and if, in exiting, these farmers sell their stock for beef thereby making new production only slowly available, only then could higher prices for some period of time be generated. This would lead to windfall gains to farmers who did not exit, until entry of new dairy operations restored equilibrium. Any farmer who recognizes that other farmers are exiting, and who expects higher prices to result, is of course less likely to exit than he would be otherwise.

Transition Problems

The most significant problems associated with implementing any of the suggested possible remedies to the problems of the current regulatory scheme are the economic problems of transition, including sociopolitical problems of equity. The possible remedies have a good deal of common ground in this regard, so that the analysis of the problems that might arise out of any remedy can be discussed collectively. Although each remedy would have a different magnitude of effect, they would all lead in the following directions:

(1) Generally lower incomes for most grade A owner-farmers outside of the Upper Midwest. On an annual basis, this amounts to about $400 a year per farmer for each $100 million saved by consumers. This burden would be primarily borne by large owner-farmers (50 percent of the burden being borne by the largest 15 percent of farmers).

(2) Higher incomes for all grade B owner-farmers, generally in the Upper Midwest.

(3) Higher incomes for all grade A farmers whose average annual blend prices exceed federal order Class II prices by 35 cents or less and possibly those whose blend prices exceed Class II prices by up to 50 cents. This would include most or all Minnesota and Wisconsin grade A farmers and very few others (with the exception of California farmers who may stand to benefit from federal order deregulation as well).

(4) Short-term losses for grade A and gains for grade B non-owner farmers or farm workers.

(5) A general decrease in the quantity of Class II milk products sold and a general decrease in the profitability of Class II processing operations initially. This decline in profitability would be strong outside the Upper Midwest. The only deviation from this conclusion is that powdered milk operations (which generally also produce butter) could possibly

become more profitable in the Upper Midwest if milk reconstitution became important. After a significant transition period, profitability should be restored to normal for these operations.

(6) Increased consumption of fluid (or reconstituted fluid) milk, increasing fluid handlers' profitability on fresh and reconstitution operations, particularly in regions located far from the Upper Midwest (excluding areas near California where the effect would be relatively small). Again, after some transition period, profitability should be restored to normal.

The primary economic problems of readjustment will be those associated with declining farm income. Farmers may overreact to declining milk prices and changing market conditions. The dissemination of information through established channels should essentially prevent this from occurring. However, if there is overreaction, supply may become restricted even more than long-run market forces would dictate, and become reestablished only after some lag.

The number of dairy farmers has been declining during the past several decades. Part of this decline is reflected in increased farm specialization and part in exit from farming altogether. The dairy industry and other industries with increasing productivity per manhour have generally experienced labor and farm exit, particularly when demand has not been increasing. The number of dairy farms in the 1940s was more than ten times that today. If they all were in production as dairy farms today with the efficiency levels of today's farms and with today's prices, they would produce enough milk to furnish most of the world's milk, if the milk could be transported rapidly enough in fluid form. Unlike the situation in industries such as aerospace, where improved technology increased employment, in the dairy industry, as in the railroad industry, greater output per manhour has led to declining employment. The response has been a form of government-sanctioned make-work or featherbedding. Featherbedding in railroads, as in farming, does not usually mean an "easy life" or worthless work product. What it does mean is that the real cost to society of some of the output is less than it is worth to consumers. Persistent declines in employment in any industry because of decreased demand or increased output per labor-hour can be painful, and methods should be found to reduce this pain. But trying to stave off advancing technology through outmoded regulation is not a proper approach. In the case of dairy farming, some farmers are kept in dairy farming who could do other work (for example, raise other agricultural commodities) that is of greater benefit to society. As is frequently suggested in such situations, undisguised payments to target groups would be less costly than the hidden make-work concepts of raising their prices (and the prices of wealthy farmers as well), to avoid what would be an even less demeaning (although perceived as more demeaning) open payment made to ease the burden of being caught in a period of technological transition.

The projected impact of the short-run increase in the decline of the number of dairy farms which one might expect as a result of deregulation (on the order of 2 percent to 5 percent measured in output terms)[25] can be softened by phased deregulation and transition payments.

In the case of deregulation, for example, this might be accomplished by letting the Class II price fall by 2 cents every other month (relative to the M-W price) over a period of eight years and four months (a 100-month period) and decreasing the fluid differential (and zone differentials) by 1 percent a month over the same period. At the end of that period, competitive premiums would probably exist on both Class I and Class II milk. All federal order Class I, Class II, and blend prices would be equal, although premium prices and premium reblends would not be equal. The final phasing out of both the Class I and the Class II prices could then be undertaken rapidly, as the classified pricing policy becomes neutral in effect because the blend price is merely the utilization average of Class I and Class II prices, which are now equal. If excessively rapid exit started to occur during this period, the M-W price would retain its corrective role by responding to raise producer prices during the phasing-out period. At the same time, USDA information dissemination on supply and prices and USDA projections would be useful adjunct policies to reduce overreaction.

Similar phased programs might be used if fluid differentials were to be lowered and if the artificial financial penalty on milk reconstitution were to be removed.

Problems of political economics might also ensue. Milk producers have in the past dumped substantial amounts of milk or killed calves to attract political attention. Such programs have generally been costly to the participants and represented an infinitesimal percent of total production. Such tactics would be likely to be employed again, however, and widely touted as examples of "disorderly marketing" and as harbingers of economic doom for the dairy farmer and the consumer.

---

[25] The exit would be higher in the South and would probably lead to some entry and expansion in the Upper Midwest. In the South, many dairy resources would be sold to the North; others would be converted to nondairy operation; and some would not be used.

These actions should be anticipated and effective counteractions should be contemplated. Counteractions include the dissemination of information about the total impact of such actions in terms of supply and prices. Also, if dumping actions involve conspiracy to defraud or conspiracy in restraint of trade, swift antitrust or other legal action should be contemplated. If these actions involve violations of supply contracts or if they involve withholding from bottlers and coercion of Class II manufacturing facilities not to resell raw milk to bottlers, then the possibility of rapid legal response should again be contemplated. Finally, in the unlikely event that withholding actions do lead to measurably higher prices traceable to the withholding action, then the order would not be achieving the goals of Congress, and removal of the order(s) involved would be an appropriate response.

One of the advantages of phased deregulation would be that no such actions could effectively continue for any extended periods of time without massive costs to participants and increased profits to nonparticipants. The other advantage is that phased deregulation will allow time for most farmers to realize that it will not hurt their incomes as much as many opponents of deregulation fear.

A final problem of transition is the political problem of equity. Higher farm prices lead to a bidding up of farm values, resulting in what are called "economic rents." A person who buys a farm in anticipation of continued regulation earns no profits from the regulations. The person who profits is the seller of the farm whose sale price is enhanced by the expected future milk price levels. Farmers who rent farms likewise benefit very little, although the landlord receives a higher rental value.

Expectations of continued government regulations certainly create no vested property rights in landowners whose assets will diminish in value if the regulation ceases. Indeed, the value of the land probably reflects the market's assessment of the probability of deregulation. Many would argue that the landowner buys at his own risk. Nonetheless, the issue is a political one to be answered by the political process. If compensation is considered appropriate, a variety of solutions exist because there is a variety of opinion about what an equitable result would be.

If the purpose of these programs is to help all farmers, rich or poor, to obtain incomes closer to those earned in other sectors of the economy, then a transition payment would be appropriate to all farm owners (with a lower payment to renters).[26] If, instead, the programs are viewed as helping poorer farmers, a transition payment could be

---

[26] Loan programs to farmers (presumably in the Upper Midwest) who wish to expand in response to higher prices could be enlarged.

maximum payment level built

fficient transition payments
rather than a "prices" policy.
ived advantage of disguising
e enormous, especially in an
ough payments may be de-
the price decline by market
r-farmer should be based on
f any deregulation act, and
ed basis, regardless of con-
ning in farming. Otherwise,
ed and inefficient operations
solidation with other farms,

[27] Older farmers whose expertise may not be easily transferable and younger ones who opt for retraining might also receive an extra subsidy.